CONTINGENT ACADEMIC LABOR

BECOME A MEMBER

new FACULTY MAJORITY

Current and forthcoming titles publishing in our
NEW FACULTY MAJORITY
series

ADJUNCT FACULTY VOICES
Cultivating Professional Development and
Community at the Front Lines of
Higher Education
Edited by Roy Fuller, Marie Kendall Brown, and
Kimberly Smith
Foreword by Adrianna Kezar

**SUPPORTING THE NEW FACULTY
MAJORITY**
Embracing Collegiality on Campus
Don Haviland, Nathan F. Alleman, and
Cara Cliburn Allen

Available Winter 2018

CONTINGENT ACADEMIC LABOR

Evaluating Conditions to Improve Student Outcomes

Daniel Davis

Series Foreword by Maria Maisto
Foreword by Adrianna Kezar

The New Faculty Majority series

STERLING, VIRGINIA

Published by Stylus Publishing, LLC.
22883 Quicksilver Drive
Sterling, Virginia 20166-2102

Library of Congress Cataloging-in-Publication-Data

Names: Davis, Daniel B., 1981- author.
Title: Contingent academic labor : evaluating conditions to improve
student outcomes / Daniel B. Davis.
Description: First edition. |
Sterling, Virginia : Stylus Publishing, 2017. |
Includes bibliographical references.
Identifiers: LCCN 2017009847 (print) |
LCCN 2017039577 (ebook) |
ISBN 9781620362532 (Library networkable e-edition) |
ISBN 9781620362549 (Consumer e-edition) |
ISBN 9781620362525 (pbk. : alk. paper) |
ISBN 9781620362518 (cloth : alk. paper)
Subjects: LCSH: College teachers, Part-time--Salaries, etc.--United
States. |
College teachers--Tenure--United States. |
Universities and colleges--United States--Faculty.
Classification: LCC LB2334 (ebook) |
LCC LB2334 .D38 2017 (print) |
DDC 378.1/25--dc23
LC record available at https://lccn.loc.gov/2017009847

13-digit ISBN: 978-1-62036-251-8 (cloth)
13-digit ISBN: 978-1-62036-252-5 (paperback)
13-digit ISBN: 978-1-62036-253-2 (library networkable e-edition)
13-digit ISBN: 978-1-62036-254-9 (consumer e-edition)

Bulk Purchases

Quantity discounts are available for use in workshops and for
staff development.
Call 1-800-232-0223

First Edition, 2017

10   9   8   7   6   5   4   3   2   1

To those who know the difference high-quality teaching makes, in hopes that many more will come to know as well.

CONTENTS

FIGURES AND TABLES

Figures

Tables

FOREWORD

This book, in my estimation, is one of the most important books focused on contingent faculty in higher education— sometimes an author hits on a concept or idea that is critical to shedding light on an issue and advancing it. We have had dozens of books outlining the problems that contingent faculty face. More recently, books outlining how these working conditions negatively impact higher education, ranging from decreased student outcomes to institutional ineffectiveness, have heightened the urgency to address this problem. Increasingly, books related to unionization as an important strategy for addressing the poor working conditions that faculty face are emerging, yet few books have advanced ideas for addressing these problematic working conditions and their impacts. Indeed, the few solutions offered to this complex issue have been overly simplistic or not robust enough to address the multitude of contexts in higher education and varying working conditions within which contingent faculty are situated. This book offers a complex tool that *does* engage the varying contexts in which different post-secondary institutions and their faculty are located. This tool is called the Contingent Labor Conditions Score.

A major concept that undergirds this tool is equity. The tool includes three different equity areas: material, professional, and social. Inequity defines most contingent faculty roles and has been the source of major critiques for the last few decades. However, much of that focus has been on material equity; this tool's strength is its multifaceted components that also address professional and social equity, areas that are often overlooked. I imagine over time that other areas may also be added or included to the tool, but these three areas are an excellent starting point for examination by institutions.

The tool offered in this book can be used by campuses that are not unionized or perhaps are unable to unionize to improve faculty working conditions. Additionally, the tool can be used by unions as a methodology to help identify areas for collective bargaining.

It might also be used to provide data to leverage discussions within collective bargaining processes. For example, if an institution is extremely low on social equity, it may be able to collectively bargain for additional resources to aid in recruiting a more diverse faculty.

This book offers important context about the rising numbers of contingent faculty namely, information about their working conditions that helps argue for the importance of the Contingent Labor Conditions Score. One of these important, unique concepts is that of "cooling out" among contingent faculty. *Cooling out* was first coined by Burton Clark (1960). He examined the experiences of students at community colleges and discovered how over time they were discouraged from furthering their education, which eventually led to their dropping out. Daniel Davis proposes a similar phenomenon is happening among contingent faculty who, as a result of their poor and inequitable working conditions, eventually dropout of the professoriate. This phenomenon helps to explain why contingent faculty enter into these employment conditions and eventually why they peter out.

In addition to the important and novel ideas offered such as the Contingent Labor Conditions Score and cooling out, this book brings an interesting voice, mixing qualitative quotes from contingent faculty members on campuses interspersed with mathematical formulas for calculating scores. This powerful mix of on-the-ground voices that express and reflect the conditions of contingent faculty on campus and the analytic calculations about how to address the problems expressed in these quotesis quite an unusual and welcomed blendof voices. On one hand, we often get a qualitative understanding of working conditions, but rarely is this paired with analytic, quantitative methods for addressing the complex problems outlined. On the other hand, we often see quantitative studies with calculation of satisfaction scores or calculations of advancement opportunities but without any voice from the faculty to understand or address these trends. It is the novel combination of different voices and data that makes this book particularly important and ground breaking.

The level of detail offered in chapter 8 about how to calculate your own score as part of the self-assessment goes beyond where most tools would go in terms of assisting campuses with addressing an issue. If I were a campus leader, I would feel I had the requisite knowledge to implement the tool and help improve the material, professional, and social equity on campus. The book also offers arguments for getting reticent colleagues to use the tool. I highly recommend this book to leaders within unions, academic administrators, and faculty leaders—both tenure-track and contingent—as *the* approach for advancing equity on college campuses because it builds off the methodology of other known tools that have advanced change in higher education like the Equity Scorecard. By having this information, campuses can propel needed action, motivate change, and identify key areas for work to improve the working conditions of contingent faculty and create a stronger teaching and learning environment for students.

Adrianna Kezar

Professor, University of Southern California

Director, The Delphi Project on the Changing Faculty and Student Success (www.thechangingfaculty.org)

SERIES FOREWORD

New Faculty Majority (NFM): The National Coalition for Adjunct and Contingent Equity was established in 2009 for one purpose: to focus on resolving the economic, ethical, political, and educational crises created by the shift to a predominantly contingent faculty workforce in higher education. The shift has occurred over decades, and it has led to an institutionalization of attitudes and policies toward contingent faculty members and toward faculty work more generally that must be described as counterproductive at best, exploitative at worst. By denying basic professional working conditions and opportunities for professional growth to faculty members without whom, ironically, higher education could not function, college and university leaders harm students and undermine the common good. Faculty working conditions are student learning conditions, so when faculty are not supported— not provided basic supports from offices to access to professional development—students are not supported. Similarly, when contingent faculty do not have academic freedom protections to ensure that they can challenge students and maintain high academic standards, they cannot fully carry out their duty to educate students to be active, responsible, discerning, courageous citizens.

This series gives members of the academic community an opportunity to wrestle with these vexing, critical issues and to explore real-world, practical, and ethical solutions. It will invite different audiences to be challenged and inspired to think; collaborate; and yes, to argue, in a way that is true to the diversity of experience that shapes us. Most important, this series will highlight the voices and perspectives of contingent faculty themselves, so that all members of the higher education community committed to quality and equity can work toward these goals with integrity and in good faith.

NFM's objective from the beginning was to create a broad coalition of constituencies including faculty, students, parents, staff, administrators, labor activists, higher education organizations, and community members who would engage in inside/outside education and advocacy. Early in its existence, NFM realized that the project it had taken on was daunting in the same way that the crisis of climate change is so frustrating; namely, that there was significant denial among people who should know better that the problem exists; it is man-made, and, therefore, it requires intentional, dedicated, and honest attention and effort to correct. This series is one important part of the effort to ensure that the climate of higher education is always as conducive to justice as it is to success.

Maria Maisto
President, New Faculty Majority

ACKNOWLEDGMENTS

Thank you to all who offered comments on this guide, including scholarly feedback from Adrianna Kezar at the University of Southern California and Amy Binder at the University of California, San Diego; strategic insights from Elizabeth Hoffman of the California Faculty Association; and editorial assistance from Sarah Burrows and Carey Blakely. Thank you to my wife, Rachel, for your constant support and for making it financially possible for me to have accepted contingent teaching roles, at times only because they felt meaningful despite the pay and conditions.

In addition, thank you to the contingent faculty members who shared your experiences, which comprise many of the meaningful quotes throughout these pages. This guide is significantly improved thanks to your input.

Introduction

Contingent faculty members at institutions of higher education often find themselves underpaid, underemployed, and undervalued by their employers. A report delivered to the U.S. House of Representatives included the following statement from a contingent faculty member, revealing an all-too-common situation encountered by the proliferating contingent ranks:

> Despite all the work I do, I earn very little. Typical compensation is approximately $2,300–$2,500 per class. In 2012, as a result of working at three institutions, my income was approximately $25,000. My husband and I live, like so many other American families, from paycheck to paycheck, praying that our only working car will not break down, that I will not get sick and be unable to work, and that we will be able to make our house payments. (House Committee on Education and the Workforce Democratic Staff, 2014, p. 7)

As the numbers of contingent faculty swell, most notably at community colleges and teaching (as opposed to research) institutions, it is vital that campus administrators and other leaders involved in hiring faculty assess their campus's strengths and growth areas in terms of how contingent faculty are treated and then make decisions accordingly. The purpose of implementing these changes is not only to cultivate employees who are more engaged and invested in the institution and their pedagogical profession but also, by extension, to improve student outcomes. Adrianna Kezar (2012), professor of higher education at the University of Southern California and prolific scholar on issues of contingent labor, writes that a first step in building on a campus's growth areas is to use "data, benchmarks, and model institutions to guide policies" (p. 38). This book is intended to aid in that process, with the central goals being awareness of the issues pertaining to the labor conditions of contingent faculty; the impacts of these conditions on contingent faculty members, their students, their campus, and their profession; and providing a means for assessing those labor conditions with the ultimate hope of

1

improving them. Arguably, by making the work environment of contingent faculty more materially, professionally, and socially equitable, campus leaders will take the important step of enhancing the learning outcomes and academic integrity of their institutions.

This book contains three sections. Part one places contingent academic labor within broader contexts, briefly situating the topic in economic, social, and higher education trends. Part two illustrates the range of academic working conditions for contingent faculty in the material, professional, and social equity categories. Part three offers and explains the Contingent Labor Conditions Score, a tool to help individual institutions assess their own contingent faculty work conditions.

A Focus on Teaching Institutions

This book focuses on institutions where the primary vocation of most faculty members is teaching rather than research. Top-tier research universities have fewer contingent faculty members than other types of postsecondary institutions. This is not only a result of their larger budgets but also because they have high numbers of graduate student teaching assistants, who in effect serve as their contingent faculty labor force. That said, although graduate student associations or graduate student unions may find value in some of the ideas in this text, it is not primarily written with graduate student teaching assistants in mind.

Part One

Contingent Academic Labor in Broader Contexts

This section situates contingent faculty labor issues in relation to larger social forces. Chapter 1 shows that many of the struggles faced by contingent faculty members are similar to those faced by contingent workers across industries. Chapter 1 also discusses economic trends behind the nationwide shift toward precarious work. Chapter 2 offers a brief review of the impact of contingent faculty's working conditions on students' learning, retention, and graduation outcomes (including their eventual financial success). Chapter 3 explains how a long-standing theory in higher education studies regarding the management of student ambition can be readily applied to contingent faculty—particularly to the emotional challenges faced by aspiring academics who do not make tenure-track lines.

1

Contingent Faculty Amid National Labor Trends

Taylor Jennings recently finished her PhD program in psychology at a state university in the Midwest. She finished with $50,000 in student loan debt and big ambitions of becoming a professor of psychology. She applied to dozens of colleges with full-time job openings, and although well qualified, she was competing against more than 100 applicants for most of the jobs, many from universities that ranked higher than hers. By the time hiring season was over, Taylor submitted her application to the adjunct pool at a couple of local community colleges and told herself she would reapply for tenure-track positions again the next year. She was able to pick up three classes for the fall semester as a contingent lecturer at two different community colleges. Each course paid about $3,000. She picked up three classes again for the spring semester at the same pay rate. Thankfully, her parents were able to help Taylor make ends meet, which was embarrassing for her because after so many years of investment in graduate school, she did not expect to spend her first year out making a paltry $18,000.

Taylor applied to many more schools for tenure-track positions the following year and expanded the geographic regions she was considering. This time she landed a few interviews, but none materialized into an offer. Again, the competition was steep, with far more PhDs on the market than full-time professorships. As the hiring season began to wind down again, she was offered an additional course as a contingent lecturer at one of her original two community colleges and a new one at a third college. She reluctantly accepted. Taylor found herself working very long hours and commuting frantically across town most days between campuses. She ended the year having earned a little more than $25,000 and again needed support from family because of her meager wages. This story repeated itself a third year, but by that time it was hard for her to juggle all the teaching responsibilities and still launch a full job-search campaign. Further, Taylor was unable to publish because of the teaching load and found her curriculum vitae, or academic résumé, beginning to grow stale. It also didn't help that new cohorts of freshly minted PhDs were competing against her each year.

Taylor still loves teaching and hopes to do research over the summer, but she will also need to teach summer school to make ends meet. Her ambition has waned because her confidence has been shaken. She notices that she gives less attention to grading and class prep and is rarely available to meet with students outside class because she often has to commute to the next campus. Taylor actively wonders how much longer she can do this. Aside from the incredible cost of time and energy that went into graduate school, let alone the resulting loan debt, she is not sure what else she could do if she left academia. For most other jobs, she would be considered overqualified and underexperienced.

Taylor's story is her own, but it is not unique. Thousands of bright and talented new graduates find themselves stuck in similar versions of this scenario. Surveys from various sources demonstrate that nearly half of all faculty members are part-time and contingent. For example, a survey conducted by the American Federation of Teachers (2010) found that "part-time adjunct faculty members account for 47% of all faculty, not including graduate employees" (p. 3), and up to 70% of the faculty at some community colleges. Additionally, a Coalition on the Academic Workforce (CAW; Coalition on the Academic Workforce, 2012) survey found that the part-time contingent workforce is more than 700,000 members strong and makes up "almost half the entire higher education faculty in the United States" (p. 2). Data from the U.S. Department of Education's Integrated Postsecondary Education Data System (IPEDS) show similar numbers, as seen in Figure 1.1. The number of part-time faculty at degree-granting institutions has risen steadily from less than one out of four faculty in 1970 to about one out of two today. But as mentioned in the American Federation of Teachers survey, the rates are not equal by type of institution.

In fact, data from the U.S. Department of Education (2016) demonstrate that there is an incredible range in the percentage of full-time faculty by institutional type. The College Scorecard reports institutional-level data rather than employee-level data, but averaging the percentage of full-time faculty among campuses of the same Carnegie Classification is still illuminating. Campuses on the low end have the Carnegie designation Special Focus Four-Year: Other Technology-Related Schools with 17% of their faculty full-time. On the high end of the scale, campuses designated Doctoral Universities: Highest Research Activity have 78% of faculty full-time. Of course research universities rely on doctoral students to act as teaching assistants for many sections of courses, diminishing their need for contingent academic labor.

The terms used to define these non-tenure-track positions are quite telling. The word *contingent* (2017) means "likely but not certain to happen,"

FIGURE 1.1. Percent of U.S. faculty working part-time by year.

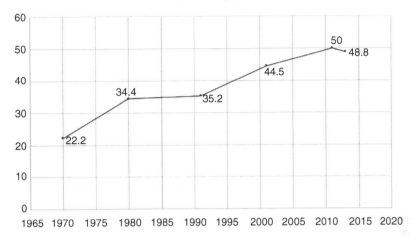

Note. From National Center for Education Statistics (2016, Table 315.10).

"not logically necessary," "subject to chance . . . unpredictable," and "dependent on or conditioned by something else." This illustrates the precarious and insecure nature of contingent academic work, subject to last-minute cuts or changes based on fluctuating enrollment numbers and departmental budgets. The word *adjunct* (2017) means "something joined or added to another thing but not essentially a part of it." This conveys the second-class treatment many adjunct faculty feel, left out of much of the decision-making and intellectual community of the campuses where they teach; in short, they are unessential add-ons. Both terms, *contingent* and *adjunct*, are often used synonymously, but this book primarily uses *contingent*, as some contingent faculty members view the word *adjunct* as pejorative. When nearly half of the teaching force is subject to change and supplemental, the integrity and legitimacy of institutions of higher education can be called into question, even before student outcomes are examined.

Categories of Contingent Faculty

Multiple typologies categorize contingent faculty into subgroups. Gappa and Leslie (1993) break them into the following four broad categories:

1. Career Enders teach contingently as a form of soft retirement or transition.

2. Specialists, Experts, and Professionals teach contingently for various reasons on top of a full-time career in a related profession.
3. Freelancers prefer part-time teaching loads to allow for other part-time work and/or domestic commitments.
4. Aspiring Academics openly aspire to leave the contingent ranks. This category includes graduate students, and it ranges from adjuncts at single institutions to freeway flyers piecing together a wage from multiple part-time contracts. (p. 48)

The CAW (2012) survey adds fascinating detail to this set of categories. The career enders category is relatively small, as only 9.1% of respondents were older than 65. In addition, the survey found the following trends, all of which point toward the fact that most contingent faculty are aspiring academics seeking full-time academic employment (Coalition on the Academic Workforce, 2012):

- 73% consider their faculty teaching role as their primary employment.
- 74% said they would take a full-time position at their current institution if given the chance.
- Only 25% prefer part-time to full-time positions.
- 50% were actively seeking or planning to seek a full-time position. (p. 9)

Furthermore, the American Federation of Teachers (AFT, 2010) survey found that 66% of participants worked two or more jobs. So although Gappa and Leslie's (1993) four categories are useful for acknowledging the diversity of situations contingent faculty may be in, the statistics show that the vast majority are aspiring academics and are not satisfied with their situation, like Taylor in this chapter's opening vignette.

Contingent faculty are found in similar numbers across age groups, with 19% aged 26 to 35, 22% aged 36 to 45, 23% aged 46 to 55, and 26% aged 56 to 65 (Coalition on the Academic Workforce, 2012, p. 19). Relatively few are under 25 or over 65. More than 80% have been teaching part-time for 3 years or more, more than 55% for 6 years or more, and more than 30% for 10 years or more (Coalition on the Academic Workforce, 2012, p. 9).

Educationally, 40% of contingent faculty have a master's degree as their highest degree, 47% have a PhD or professional doctorate, and another 7% are still finishing their doctorates. Only 6% did not have a graduate degree (Coalition on the Academic Workforce, 2012, p. 23). Institutionally, 39% teach at two-year colleges, 36% at baccalaureate and master's institutions, and 22% at doctoral and research institutions (Coalition on the Academic Workforce, 2012, p. 7). The AFT (2010) survey found similar numbers.

Generally, faculty without doctorates are limited to community colleges and smaller four-year campuses.

In short, contingent faculty members make up a highly educated workforce with significant teaching experience. They are spread across age ranges and institution types but unified in that most share a desire to move into a more secure full-time position.

Precarious Labor Is Growing Across Sectors

Precarious employment consists of jobs that lack long-term security and stability and, therefore, includes all forms of contract-based, temporary, gig, and contingent work. The shift away from full-time employment with longevity at a single place of employment is a long-term trend in the labor economy in the United States (Kalleberg, 2011) and globally (Standing, 2011). It is not a short-term fluctuation nor is the academic market unique in its shift toward precariousness. This move from secure, well-compensated jobs to part-time contract work has its roots in a web of complex social, political, and economic shifts, including but not limited to the following:

- market deregulation, which weakens workers' legal protections
- the multidecade decline in American labor movement strength, which makes workers more vulnerable to poor working conditions
- increasing global competition, which incentivizes employers to cut costs any way possible
- decreased, or at least uneven, state funding of public institutions
- a growing and diversifying labor pool, which causes more workers to compete against each other, leading to conditions that tend to favor the employer
- technological advances that automate many jobs previously requiring full-time employees
- the rise of the temporary work economy, with companies like Uber and Airbnb disrupting industries that typically employ full-time staff
- the Great Recession, which was used to justify significant changes to labor conditions that otherwise may not have been accepted by the stakeholders involved

In addition, economists note that economic inequality has been mounting for decades, largely because, as Thomas Pikkety (2014) points out, wage increases have stagnated compared to the growth of returns on capital. In other words, those whose incomes are dependent on their work have found themselves with flagging opportunities, whereas those whose incomes are dependent on their investments have seen growing returns. This has been accelerated in the United States by changes to the types of work available, with fewer upper-working-class and lower-middle-class jobs as a proportion of overall jobs than in previous decades. As manufacturing jobs have been largely outsourced to other nations, they have been replaced by lower-paying service, retail, and temporary work as well as by higher-paying technology and management jobs. Companies with large market shares, like Amazon and Starbucks, make it difficult for small businesses in the same sectors to compete. Working in upper management or in a technology role in one of these large companies usually pays quite well, but on the other end of the spectrum, warehouse workers and baristas do not tend to be highly compensated. Companies increasingly prefer employment arrangements based on contract or gig work because of the cost savings to the company, despite the job insecurity passed on to those working for them (Davis, 2016).

These trends are contributing to a polarization in the U.S. labor landscape, with some growth in upper-level jobs and large growth in lower-level jobs (Kalleberg, 2011). Similar processes are at work in higher education. Well-compensated full-time administrative positions are multiplying as are low-paid contingent instructional roles. This "rapidly growing temporary help industry" (Milner & Pinker, 2001, p. 1046) raises a variety of new challenges in labor contracting (Milner & Pinker, 2001), employee management (Lautsch, 2002), worker commitment (Linden, Wayne, Kraimer, & Sparrowe, 2003), legal protections and rights (Smith, 2008), and more.

The Role of Labor Movements

The labor movement has been weakened over the past several decades, as illustrated by a decline in labor union density across the globe (Lerner, 2009). One measure of this weakening labor movement in the United States is the rapid drop-off in strike activity. As one labor scholar writes, "Strike participation is a more rigorous indicator of individual values than a vote or union resolution or an answer to a survey question, for here one sees people sacrificing income, perhaps putting their jobs at risk" (Haydu, 1988, p. 25). Table 1.1 shows the frequency of strikes with at least 1,000 participants, dropping from more than 350 annually in the 1950s to an average of 15 strikes per year in the second decade of the twenty-first century.

Along the same lines, over the past half century, U.S. "union membership in the private sector fell from over 30 percent to less than 10 percent" (Fantasia & Stepan-Norris 2007). One sector going against this general trend, however, is higher education.

TABLE 1.1
Number of U.S. Strikes by Decade

Decade	Average Number of Strikes Annually	Average Number of Workers Involved Annually
2010–2016	14.6	77,300
2000s	20.1	128,300
1990s	34.7	207,900
1980s	83.1	506,600
1970s	288.8	1,487,800
1960s	282.9	1,233,700
1950s	351.7	1,588,400

Note. Only strikes involving 1,000 people or more are recorded. Adapted from U.S. Department of Labor, Bureau of Labor Statistics (2016).

In 2012 about 25% of all U.S. faculty members were unionized, with 41% of faculty at public community colleges belonging to unions (Berry & Savaris, 2012). An estimated 147,021 contingent faculty were represented by unions in 2012, a number that had nearly doubled over a decade (Berry & Savaris, 2012). Berry and Savaris (2012) noted that 54% of organized faculty are represented by one of three national unions: the American Association of University Professors (AAUP), the AFT, and the National Education Association (NEA).

In private four-year universities, only 3% of full-time faculty and 8% of part-time faculty are unionized (Berry & Savaris, 2012). These low rates are a result of *National Labor Relations Board v. Yeshiva University* (1980), in which the Supreme Court found faculty at private universities to be managers and thus excluded from the ability to unionize. However, Rhoades (1998) argues that faculty members are indeed managed professionals rather than managers and are thus worthy of unionization. Only recently have private university faculty begun to challenge the more than three decades old ruling (e.g., at Pacific Lutheran University [Jaschik, 2015]).

Faculty members have led the way in the move toward unionization over the past few decades (Aronowitz, 1998). Historically, faculty groups such as the AAUP were against unionization, seeing it as a contradiction to the professional status of the field. In view of the eroding power of faculty relative to administrations, the AAUP changed to support unionization in the 1970s despite great internal debate resulting in the eventual loss of about 20% of its members (McHenry & Sharkey, 2014). According to DeCew (2003), debates among many faculty groups, particularly the most elite, find unionization incompatible with fundamental academic values. Wickens (2008) surveyed literature on university labor unions. Although no panacea, the author noted modest salary gains at two-year universities and significantly improved job security. Wickens also predicted that unionization would continue to expand across U.S. campuses for the foreseeable future and lamented the dearth of research on the topic. The following year, in 2009, the peer-reviewed *Journal of Collective Bargaining in the Academy* was launched, slowly building this body of scholarship. Wickens was right about the continued union spread among faculty; for example, Bertoncini and Dorer (2016) reported that 35 private colleges unionized their contingent faculty between the 2013–2014 and 2015–2016 academic years.

It appears that although unions have generally been losing influence over the past several decades, higher education faculty are increasingly turning to them as a way to challenge their deteriorating employment conditions.

How Contingent Faculty Frame Their Situation

The previous three sections of this chapter discuss structural factors influencing faculty equity. This section looks at a key cultural element—how people narratively frame the situation of faculty labor conditions. For example, consider the language of exploitation. Documentation of part-time faculty expressing experiences of exploitation is not new and is, in fact, proliferating (a sampling across the decades includes Berry, 2005; Buckley, Healy, & Ziv, 1985; Carroll, 2003; Gappa, 1984; Karmen, 1978; Zobel, 2009). Gulli (2009) even characterizes contingent faculty as being superexploited.

In discussing this exploitation, contingent faculty members have also employed divergent discourses. Most commonly, frames have ranged from justice-oriented, compensation-equity frames (i.e., equal pay for equal work) to learning-oriented, student-benefit frames (i.e., faculty working conditions are student learning conditions.). The use of victimization frames is growing and has regularly included metaphors of migrant wage laborers (Baldwin & Chronister, 2001; Jay, 2004; McConnell, 1993; Mysyk, 2001), a lower caste of untouchables (McHenry & Sharkey, 2014), and even domestic violence (Bousquet, 2005). As overreaching as some of these frames may be, they represent a desire to highlight the situation as dire, urgent, and in desperate need of change. Consider the following opposing frames that are routinely marshaled in the debate on contingent faculty conditions.

Frame A: Contingency as Voluntary, Flexible, and Empowering

Typical discourses discounting exploitation assume that contingent faculty members hold primary jobs from which they presumably derive a sense of professional identity, stable wages, and essential benefits; therefore, they should not be reliant on their contingent employment for these professional features (Yang & Zak, 1981). Examples abound, such as the information technology manager by day who teaches a computing class at night for the associated prestige; the stay-at-home parent teaching a class to keep a toe in the professional world; the graduate student picking up a class to build valuable teaching experience while finishing a degree; and the full-time professor moonlighting at another institution to pay for his or her children's college tuition. In this frame, part-time contingent teaching is voluntary and flexible employment, intended to supplement another vocation in a meaningful way.

Frame B: Contingency as Exploitation

Counterarguments often point to the *freeway flyers*, defined as contingent faculty members struggling to scratch together an existence from contingent contracts at multiple institutions. These faculty depend on summer unemployment benefits, hope their car (doubling as an office) does not break down, and seek and wish for full-time academic employment. This frame then goes on to describe how contingent faculty members do not receive the same respect given to their tenure-track colleagues. Contingent faculty also do not have access to health and retirement benefits, job security, a seat at the table of shared governance, or institutional support services (e.g., administrative support, travel budgets, and development training). Usually, this argument is further bolstered with evidence that part-time instructors are growing as a share of the academic workforce; indeed, on some campuses they are the majority of instructional employees. Additionally, for contingent faculty members whose source of vocational identity hinges on their academic position, not only is their job insecure but their entire vocational and professional identity has likewise become contingent. Their income is often close to or below the poverty level, a problem greatly exacerbated if there are dependents in the household. Insecure employment is wounding to professional self-esteem and self-confidence, insofar as one's vocation is linked to one's sense of identity. In this frame, contingent teaching is deeply exploitative, materially and psychologically. It also has negative spillover effects for student learning, discussed in chapter 2.

Each of these frames tells a portion of the story. Both are valid perspectives that largely depend on one's circumstances. Interviews of contingent faculty members reveal that their experiences fall across a spectrum between these poles (Kezar, 2013; chapters 4–6, this book). Faculty members' work-life situations and the personal reasons they have for taking on contingent employment are myriad. This is why differing sides, by thinking of contingent faculty as a homogenous group, can so easily talk past each other. The Contingent Labor Conditions Score introduced in part three helps avoid this kind of either/or framing for a more nuanced and accurate picture of the situation at each institution.

Overall, the plight of contingent faculty, although unique in many features, is not wholly dissimilar to challenges faced by many professionals in industries increasingly using a more flexible workforce. One marked difference, however, is that although union participation is down in most other industries, it is on the uptick in academia. Another unique challenge is that the narrative frames used to explain the situation vary substantially from voluntary and empowered to exploited and marginalized, with little in between. Chapter 2 moves away from the broader social issues surrounding contingent academics to focus on how contingent faculty members' work conditions influence student outcomes.

2

The Influence of Contingent Faculty Work Conditions on Student Outcomes

Studies examining the impact of contingent faculty on students focus on a variety of different outcomes. Ochoa's (2012) literature review offers three outcome categories: student learning, student persistence, and graduation rates. Each of these outcome types can be broken down further into subtypes. For example, "Persistence can mean taking another course in a subject, continuing on to the next semester or year, or [not] dropping a class" (Ochoa, 2012, p. 142). In addition, the type of institution plays a role because conditions vary across institution types. Factors like campus resources and endowment size, quality of professional development and evaluation, pay rates and job security of contingent faculty, unionization, extent of use of graduate teaching assistants, campus use of full-time non-tenure-track contingent faculty, and more all play a part in shaping the effectiveness of contingent educators compared with tenure-track faculty members.

Measuring actual learning outcomes is notoriously difficult, and large-scale attempts have shown underwhelming results across the country (Arum & Roksa, 2011). One difficulty in measuring learning is that the concept itself can be broken into a variety of analytical, cognitive, and even cultural skills. Mueller, Mandernach, and Sanderson (2013) simply compared student grades across different sections of an online university foundations course in which some sections were taught by adjuncts and others by tenure-track faculty. The students in the courses taught by adjuncts scored slightly lower. Of course, the opposite situation can also be the case; Sonner (2000) found that contingent faculty are under greater pressure to inflate grades because of their greater need for strong student evaluations compared to faculty with more secure employment arrangements. This is simply because poor student evaluations can be more threatening to contingent faculty members who fear not getting rehired if students complain. It becomes rational to appease students with slightly less rigorous grading standards, although in the long run this diminishes the quality of education provided.

Grade inflation notwithstanding, Figlio, Schapiro, and Soter (2015) found an interesting outcome at Northwestern University, where contingent faculty have notably higher job security and more equitable treatment than at most other institutions. In this study, freshmen who took introductory classes from non-tenure-track faculty went on to score higher in subsequent courses in that major than the students who were taught by tenure-track faculty. This finding should not be terribly surprising, given that when a faculty member focuses on pedagogy over research, that shift of priority can be expected to yield dividends for students. But in most other contexts where contingent faculty have less professional standing than at Northwestern, the data point toward students performing better when taking classes from tenure-track faculty.

The evidence for student retention and completion is more direct than learning outcomes. Bettinger and Long (2004) found that students are less likely to persist in a major after exposure to contingent faculty. Eagan and Jaeger (2008) noted that first-year students in gateway courses taught by contingent faculty are less likely to stay at the institution for their second year. One slight aberration is Hutto's (2013) finding that students at one community college had slightly higher course retention when taught by adjuncts but then concluded that grade inflation among adjuncts was a chief contributing factor. Jacoby (2006) reported that community colleges with higher contingent faculty ratios have lower graduation rates, whereas Ehrenberg and Zang (2005) reported that public four-year campuses also have modestly declining graduation rates as the ratio of contingent faculty increases. Put simply, most campuses do not have great conditions for their contingent faculty. As a result the overreliance on instructional labor that is not well compensated or job secure leads to worse outcomes for students. But at Northwestern University, a campus that treats contingent faculty relatively well, contingent faculty outperform more research-oriented faculty.

To avoid painting an overly simple picture, not every study has reached the same outcome. For example, Deutsch's (2015) study did not achieve statistical significance between contingent faculty and student retention, but the author noted that more than half of retention studies do find a relationship. The point is that contingent faculty members' impact on students is not a question that can be answered apart from contextual factors, namely, conditions related to how those contingent faculty members are treated. The question, therefore, is not, "How do contingent faculty members affect students?", as if contingent faculty were a monolithic group. The question is, "How do the labor conditions of contingent faculty influence student outcomes?"

In sum, mounting evidence does suggest that when contingent faculty members work under poor labor conditions, students are negatively affected. Although no evidence exists suggesting that contingent faculty members as a group are worse teachers or less qualified instructors, Umbach's (2007) study of 132 colleges and universities found that non-tenure-track or part-time faculty "interact with students less frequently, use active and collaborative techniques less often, [and] spend less time preparing for class than their tenured and tenure-track peers" (p. 110). These pedagogical practices take more time and investment, which is not feasible for the rate of pay most contingent faculty receive.

Cotton and Wilson's (2006) qualitative study of student-faculty interactions contains the following comment from a student about the limited availability of part-time faculty: "Where are they? They're not here. I don't think I have a professor this semester that's full-time faculty; they're all part-time. They show up, teach a class, then run away as soon as they can" (p. 504).

Contingent faculty regularly have other jobs and sometimes classes at multiple campuses. Contingent faculty are not often given designated office space, so they are much less present on campus than their full-time peers. This creates problems for students who benefit from more regular faculty-student interaction, especially across semesters, when long-term relationships can be built. Lower institutional commitment to contingent faculty (e.g., pay, job security, and office space) leads to worse student outcomes. This is not because contingent faculty have less ability or fewer credentials; rather, they simply are not supported well enough to elicit peak performance. In any industry, when employees feel underpaid and overworked, decreases in productivity and work quality are to be expected (Linden, Wayne, Kraimer, & Sparrowe, 2003). Yet in colleges where contingent faculty members work under better labor conditions, students may actually benefit more from contingent faculty than tenure-track faculty because contingent faculty tend to be more focused on their teaching than professors with research publication pressures (Figlio, Schapiro, & Soter, 2015).

Continued research is still needed, but strong implications exist for the usefulness of contingent faculty labor conditions as a variable in explaining student outcomes. Thus, a tool like the Contingent Labor Conditions Scorecard, described in part three, helps shed light on how to maximize gains for students because the quantitative scores on the report card can be added to statistical models in future institutional research.

Relationship Between Contingent Faculty and Students' Postcollege Earnings

Although the studies cited in this chapter focus on how students do while they are in college as a result of exposure to contingent faculty, no studies have looked at how students fare after they graduate. After paying so much in tuition, likely taking on substantial student loans, what was the return on investment to the student? The following analysis mixes publicly available data collected from the NCES (2016) and the U.S. Department of Education's (2016) College Scorecard Data to determine how the ratio of full-time versus part-time faculty affects student earnings a decade after they enroll.

Variables

The NCES's IPEDS collects the ratio of full-time faculty to overall faculty at each postsecondary institution. Although some part-time tenure-track faculty exist, their numbers are sufficiently small that the full-time to all-faculty ratio still serves as a strong proxy for an institution's reliance on contingent faculty. Carnegie Classifications (IPEDS variable name: CCBASIC) were used to select campuses for the following analysis (categories 1–10 for community colleges and 15–22 for four-year campuses), excluding special focus campuses (e.g., seminaries, trade schools, and medical schools) and hybrid cases (e.g., four-year campuses that predominantly award two-year degrees).

The U.S. Department of Education's (2016) new College Scorecard Data collects student earnings information from Internal Revenue Service data several years after students first enroll in a given college or university. Because this information is now available to the public, these two variables can now be compared.

For this analysis, a student's mean earnings 10 years after initially enrolling in college were used, based on Internal Revenue Service data from 2014. The College Scorecard Data documentation defines *earnings* as "the sum of wages and deferred compensation from all non-duplicate W-2 forms received for each individual, plus positive self-employment earnings from Schedule SE [self-employment]" (U.S. Department of Education, 2016, p. 16). Studies of graduation rates tend to show that roughly equal proportions of undergraduates at four-year colleges and universities finish in four, five, and six years. Thus, the full-time faculty ratio applied was the mean average for the successive six years after students enrolled, or the 2004–2005 academic year through the 2009–2010 academic year. For two-year colleges, a similar 150% time to completion strategy was numerically implemented, creating a full-time faculty ratio that is a mean of the 2004–2005 academic year through the 2006–2007 academic year.

Nonaccredited institutions, non-degree-granting institutions, institutions outside the 50 U.S. states or the District of Columbia (e.g., Guam, Puerto Rico), and branch or satellite sites of other campuses were not included in the analysis.

Results and Implications

For community colleges, the full-time faculty ratio was broken into five quintiles, or campuses, organized according to the percentage of full-time faculty. For each percentage range, the mean student income 10 years after enrollment (*M*) is shown in Table 2.1 as well as the standard deviation (*SD*).

An analysis of variance (ANOVA) analyzing 1,188 community college campuses revealed that a statistically significant relationship exists between the mean ratio of faculty who were full-time between the 2004–2005 and 2006–2007 academic years, and students' average earnings 10 years after first enrollment in 2014 [$F(4,1187) = 2.907$, $p = 0.021$]. See Figure 2.1 for a visual representation.

It is worth noting that although the income drops in the fourth quintile, or among two-year campuses with between 60% and 80% full-time faculty, this is likely because of an overrepresentation of for-profit campuses. Of the 217 campuses that fell in that quadrant, 146 of them, or 67%, were for profit.

As a point of comparison, according to the U.S. Census Bureau (n.d.a.), in 2014 median household income was $53,482, and per capita individual income was $28,555. College-educated people make at least slightly more— even from campuses with low ratios of full-time faculty—than those who received no higher education at all (U.S. Census Bureau, n.d.a.).

TABLE 2.1

Student Income by Quintile of Full-Time Faculty Ratio at Two-Year Campuses

Quintile of Full-Time Faculty During Years of Enrollment	Mean Student Income 10 Years Post-Enrollment	Standard Deviation
0% to 20% of the faculty are full-time	$31,453.75	$5,330.33
20.1% to 40% of the faculty are full-time	$33,185.16	$5,154.66
40.1% to 60% of the faculty are full-time	$33,180.97	$7,977.42
60.1% to 80% of the faculty are full-time	$32,493.38	$8,049.22
80.1% to 100% of the faculty are full-time	$34,426.76	$8,502.41

Note. Data from U.S. Department of Education's (2016) College Scorecard Data. Analysis by Davis.

FIGURE 2.1. Two-year campuses: Ratio of full-time faculty to student earnings.

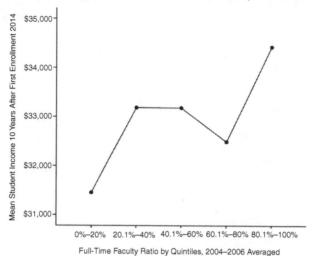

Full-Time Faculty Ratio by Quintiles, 2004–2006 Averaged

Note. Data from U.S. Department of Education's (2016) College Scorecard Data. Analysis by Davis.

For four-year campuses, the full-time faculty ratio was also broken into quintiles as shown in Table 2.2.

TABLE 2.2
Student Income by Quintile of Full-Time Faculty Ratio at Four-Year Campuses

Quintile of Full-Time Faculty During Years of Enrollment	Mean Student Income 10 Years Post-Enrollment	Standard Deviation
0% to 20% of the faculty are full-time	$44,304.65	$10,091.63
20.1% to 40% of the faculty are full-time	$45,125.00	$8,028.08
40.1% to 60% of the faculty are full-time	$46,701.27	$9,949.22
60.1% to 80% of the faculty are full-time	$46,728.74	$12,074.91
80.1% to 100% of the faculty are full-time	$49,082.34	$15,059.23

Note. Data from U.S. Department of Education's (2016) College Scorecard Data. Analysis by Davis.

Similar to two-year community colleges, an ANOVA applied to 1,411 four-year campuses also revealed that a statistically significant relationship exists between the mean ratio of faculty who were full-time between the

FIGURE 2.2. Four-year campuses: Ratio of full-time faculty to student earnings.

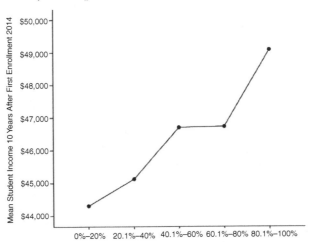

2004–2005 and 2009–2010 academic years, and students' average earnings in 2014 [$F(4,1410) = 4.671$, $p = 0.001$]. These include all accredited degree-granting four-year institutions in the United States, excluding those awarding mostly two-year degrees or special focus colleges like seminaries and law schools (see Figure 2.2).

Although the relationships shown in Figure 2.1 and Figure 2.2 may not be completely independent of other variables—like the resource level of an institution or student backgrounds when applying—they nevertheless imply that students who attend colleges with a low percentage of full-time faculty have lower income prospects years later. With these data now publicly available, it may not be long before students begin to look at full-time faculty ratios in addition to other long-used indicators of value, such as class sizes, student-to-teacher ratios, graduation rates, tuition costs, and so on, when making their college choices. Finally, although the statistical analysis presented here is not a predictive model, it does fit the hypothesis one would expect based on the literature reviewed in the first half of this chapter.

More than ever, campus administrators would do well to track their contingent labor conditions and consider the ratio of full- to part-time faculty they wish to have. Terri, a contingent faculty member teaching at three different campuses in San Diego who was interviewed for this book, expressed the nuances of the problem well.

> I love my students, and I care about doing a good job. But to make ends meet I have to teach at least 10 classes a year, which is more than I should. I'm forced to go for quantity over quality. I end up trading writing assignments

for [online] multiple-choice quizzes. I don't get to mentor students how I want; in some cases I don't even get to know their names. I get nervous to talk about hot topics in class because I can't afford a frustrated student to bad-mouth me to the chair or dean, which shouldn't matter because you would think they should side with faculty, but I don't know [the chair or dean] enough and they don't know me enough to trust me over the student. I don't get to update my material every semester because I'm usually always playing catch up on grading. I hate that I feel like I'm cutting corners. The students lose out, I lose out, and I would say even the campus's brand is tarnished because I'm not the only one who has to compromise. I don't understand why this situation persists when it's a lose-lose-lose scenario. There has to be a better way.

Administrators can use their Contingent Labor Conditions Score (discussed in chapters 7 and 8; see blank forms in the Appendix or digitally at https://sty.presswarehouse.com/books/BookDetail.aspx?productID=412424) along with their full-time faculty ratio to monitor and make hiring decisions for the benefit of students, as well as the campus's own reputation. Campuses that pay their faculty more and provide greater security end up with educators more willing to assign rigorous material and coach and mentor their students to face the challenge. This in turn appears to have marketplace value for students after they graduate, reflected in an earnings premium.

3

The Cooling-Out Function on Contingent Faculty

Burton Clark, the University of California, Los Angeles's long-renowned professor of higher education, applied the concept of the cooling-out function to higher education. His original article (Clark, 1960) opens with the following statement: "A major problem of democratic society is inconsistency between encouragement to achieve and the realities of limited opportunity" (p. 569).

Clark's (1960) work examines the tension between a society that promotes college for all and a career system that sharply rations opportunity, creating a situation in which members of broad swaths of society are encouraged to seek four-year degrees, promised they are part of the American dream, and seemingly ensured a path to middle-class success. But at the same time, many of these graduates are systematically denied access to the career opportunities that would fulfill such promises. The U.S. social structure does not allow everyone to attain high-paying and prestigious occupations; thus, many are steered toward lesser opportunities. Their ambitions are originally heated up, but then must be cooled out.

At the time of Clark's (1960) writing, community colleges were just beginning to proliferate and became the main focus of his analysis. Of course the cooling-out function happens at four-year institutions as well, but according to Clark, community colleges especially serve to manage ambition. The idea has continued to spark debate and research (e.g., Alexander, Bozick, & Entwisle, 2008; Bahr, 2008; Rosenbaum, Deil-Amen, & Person, 2006).

Clark's (1960) application of the term *cooling out* is a reference to sociologist Erving Goffman's (1952) article in which he looks at the work of confidence (con) artists who identify a mark or victim for their con. They invite the mark to be a partner in a scheme as a way to make an easy profit. The mark gets up the nerve and invests. After some initial return, the mark is drawn to invest a greater amount. Suddenly, because of a mistake, the mark's entire investment is lost. At this point the operators leave the mark a "little wiser and a lot poorer" (Goffman, 1952, p. 451). However, not all marks are willing to accept their losses and move on; some will go to the police or spread their frustration to other potential marks, which is bad business for the operators. Thus the operators will often leave a member behind, the cooler, who attempts to

> keep the anger of the mark within manageable and sensible proportions. . . . The mark is given instruction in the philosophy of taking a loss . . . to talk him into a point of view from which it is possible to accept a loss. In essence, then, the cooler has the job of handling persons who have been caught out on a limb—persons whose expectations and self-conceptions have been built up and then shattered. The mark is a person who has compromised himself, in his own eyes if not in the eyes of others. (Goffman, 1952, p. 452)

The cooling-out function, therefore, is a practice in the "art of consolation" (Goffman, 1952, p. 452). Goffman goes on to note that although situations with actual con artists are restricted to a few social settings, people who have had parallel experiences of structured disappointment are found in many contexts, or as Goffman explains it, "Cooling the mark out is one theme in a very basic social story" (p. 453). This is where Burton Clark (1960) extends the idea into community colleges and traces key mechanisms that reenact this same process in the context of students. Although Clark describes students in the following excerpt, his words provide a hauntingly appropriate summary of the situation facing contingent faculty:

> In summary, the cooling-out process in higher education is one whereby systematic discrepancy [exists] between aspirations and avenue. . . . The provision of readily available alternative achievements in itself is an important device for alleviating the stress consequent on failure and so preventing anomic and deviant behavior. The general result of cooling-out processes is that society can continue to encourage maximum effort without major disturbance from unfulfilled promises and expectations. (p. 576)

In this chapter I argue that the mechanisms Clark (1960) identified for cooling out students are parallel to the ones used to cool out aspiring faculty, particularly through the use of contingent faculty roles.

Of course Goffman (1952) and Clark (1960) are not the only sociologists to tackle such issues. Randall Collins (1979) warns about *credential inflation*, or the overproduction of degrees and the resulting increase in degree requirements for jobs that previously did not require them. Collins argues that this leads to a situation in which holders of degrees no longer have secure assurance of positions that decades before might have been a reasonable assumption; thus, those with graduate degrees find their master's or doctorate less likely to land them full-time secure academic appointments. Consider as well the current hiring shift at many community colleges, which increasingly favor applicants with a doctoral degree even though only a master's is required. Pierre Bourdieu warns that a "structural mismatch between aspirations and real probabilities" occurs as graduates' identity and self-image have been falsely elevated and then "undermined by a social . . . and educational system that has fobbed them off with worthless paper [i.e., degrees]," and those college graduates end up as "factory workers or postmen" (Bourdieu & Passeron 1979, p. 84).

Fifty years later in the United States, credential inflation remains highly problematic. A deep psychological trauma takes place for the aspiring faculty whose sense of identity and self-image has been elevated as a result of hard work in graduate school, only to find the professoriate largely out of reach. In its place, alternate paths of precarious academic piecework have come to exist, which no doubt create disillusionment and anger, as the comments throughout this book clearly reveal. But because a portion of aspiring academics will not simply accept their loss quietly, as Goffman (1952) notes of the marks in con artists' schemes, a structured cooling-out system is critical to manage anger and lower ambitions. To accept the loss of a full-time academic appointment would be to abandon visions of the professoriate shortly after failing to attain the desired appointment and reorient oneself to a career in *industry*—the term academics use for the general job market. This is a bitter pill to swallow for those who have put so much into their academic vision and who have been socialized to see the professoriate as the truest measure of professional success, never mind the fact that many employers view PhD holders as overqualified and yet lacking in experience, a dismal combination. As a result, a large proportion of those who do not land permanent academic appointments accept contingent appointments in hopes of somehow converting them into tenure-track positions. Such job conversions happen often enough for many contingent faculty members to justify their hopes and willingness to linger in their contingent positions but not often enough to match the ambitions of most contingent faculty.

The Mechanisms of Cooling Out

Year after year contingent faculty members who do not get their hoped-for full-time positions must decide whether to stay in academia or throw in the towel. On the one hand, each new year brings another batch of fresh graduates who directly compete with them for jobs, and at the same time their résumés grow longer with contingent teaching experience, viewed negatively by many hiring committees when contingency is of long duration. On the other hand, the sunke costs from holding out for a better position make leaving even more painful to face; plus, many long-term contingent faculty members may not have continued developing other marketable skills. Ultimately, contingent faculty face situations eerily parallel to the mechanisms Clark (1960) identified in his article about cooling out students.

Alternate Achievement

Substitute avenues are offered as not all that different from what is given up, although they are certainly lower in status. For Clark's (1960) community college students, this consisted of moving them off a transfer track to a vocational, remedial, or extended-education track; a dental hygienist instead of dentist, paralegal instead of lawyer, and so on. For faculty today, this comes in the form of shifting them off the tenure track—into contingent appointments. One is still "faculty" and even called "professor" by students, but the academic profession is not fully embodied in these roles.

Gradual Disengagement

This is achieved through a series of small steps that slowly stall progress toward the original goal and encourage self-assessment or second-guessing as a result of shaken confidence. For contingent faculty, this may apply to extended postdocs, multiple one- and two-year visiting scholar jobs, or repeated years of freeway-flyer teaching assignments. Every passing year raises more unsettling questions about the goal, the pathway to it, and one's own self-efficacy. There is no single moment of hot rejection, only a slow cooling out of ambition.

Objective Denial

Evidence of personal failure accumulates, which allows self-confrontation by the facts rather than the direct rejection of the individual by the organization. For faculty, many years as an adjunct is itself evidence of professional shortcomings on the curriculum vitae to hiring committees, along with a limited publishing record, few grants landed, or poor teaching evaluations. When any of these blemishes accrue, which is nearly impossible to avoid in a prolonged contingent role, the outcome is a less than impressive curriculum vitae. This is, in turn, framed as an objective result of the applicant's personal shortcomings rather than as a result of the organizational structures in play. Thus, blame is shifted from the organization to the individual.

Agents of Consolation

The overambitious community college students in Clark's (1960) study were required to meet with school counselors who worked to shift their intentions. For contingent faculty, the existence of such agents of consolation are less explicit and often take the form of tenure-track faculty members, administrative colleagues, or even friends and family who may kindly suggest that they redefine success or look for different goals.

Avoidance of Standards

Rather than offering objective measures of success or failure, standards are relative to classification. Systems with a hard yes or no outcome (like applying for a single job opening) often carry a reasonably clear set of criteria for success or failure. In contrast, systems that have softer outcomes (like applying to an unpaid internship with no hard cap on the number of positions available) tend to avoid clear criteria, favoring a more ambiguous valuation of different types of ability. Ambiguous standards are particularly insidious because they sound kind at first. For contingent faculty, the nebulous set of criteria for promotion is found all along the path to a full-time position. Imagine if there were clear criteria instead, like a written expectation of five years of contingent service with positive teaching evaluations and three refereed publications. Although some would not make the cut and would feel the pain of a swift rejection, many more would rise to the occasion. Unfortunately, that would mean that more faculty would meet the requirements than a college could accommodate.

In the face of ambiguous expectations, it is never entirely clear to contingent faculty if they should try to attend every faculty meeting, speak up, and make their presence felt in the department. Should they write for grants, publish, and try to recruit student research assistants? Should they challenge students rigorously; grade with firm standards; hunt plagiarism; and, as a consequence, fail some students? The unclear yet lower expectations for contingent faculty can contribute to lower learning outcomes, thereby helping to legitimize the treatment of contingent faculty as second class. In this way the two-tier structure is reified. Yet contingent faculty are still told they are very important in the regular form e-mails sent by administrators, the annual luncheon celebrating their work, and the occasional teaching award designated for a part-time faculty member. However, success in the lower tier does not imply or offer clear entrance to the upper tier. Standards are more ambiguous. This leaves contingent faculty in a state of limbo, with no clear pathway up or out.

Cooled-Out Faculty

The culminating effect of this series of mechanisms is summed up well by Clark (1960), applied here to community college students:

> This sequence of procedures is a specific process of cooling-out; its effect, at the best, is to let down hopes gently and unexplosively. Through it students who are failing or barely passing find their occupational and academic future being redefined. Along the way, teacher-counselors urge the latent terminal student to give up his plan of transferring and stand ready to console him in accepting a terminal curriculum. The drawn-out denial when it is effective is in place of a personal, hard "No"; instead, the student is brought to realize, finally, that it is best to ease himself out of the competition to transfer. (p. 574)

The contingent faculty role runs parallel to the cooled-out community college student role described by Clark. Contingent faculty are not directly told in a single pronouncement by an official source to give up visions of the professoriate. Instead, the aspiring contingent faculty member, like Clark's students, finds his or her "occupational and academic future being redefined," and this frustrated contingent faculty member must then either accept long-term precarious employment or realize that it is best to ease out of the competition. Hacker and Dreifus (2011) write, "Some contingents love teaching so much that they'll do it with dignity and care, regardless of low pay. It's sad that their passion for the classroom is so readily exploited" (p. 59). This eventually leads to sentiments like those from adjunct Matthew Williams in Akron, Ohio, who acknowledges, "I need to get out of what I'm doing right now before I paint myself into a corner" (Hacker & Dreifus, 2011, p. 53).

Administrators also have a role in this. They can continue upholding a system that treats contingent labor as grist for the mill, grinding out cohort after cohort of contingent faculty. Year after year new sets of graduates will take contingent positions hoping that they will lead to something more permanent. But year after year the college will have to carefully maintain a system of ambition management, lest administrators find the cooling-out function is not working effectively enough and contingent faculty members' feelings of hot rejection and resentment transform into fuel for mobilization, union activity, and media publicity.

Instead, administrators can evaluate the treatment of their contingent academic workforce through the use of tools like the Contingent Labor Conditions Score (laid out in part three) and strive to improve contingent working conditions and expectations. By doing so, their contingent workforce will become more engaged, have longer retention, and be more satisfied, which all have a positive effect on student success.

Part Two

Illustrating the Range of Work Conditions

I n the following three chapters, representations of faculty experiences at institutions with contingent labor conditions falling across the spectrum are provided. Chapter 4 looks at dimensions of material equity, such as pay parity, job security, and benefits. Chapter 5 deals with faculty members' experiences of professional equity, or opportunities for professional development and advancement. Chapter 6 examines social equity as it pertains to contingent faculty diversity across race and gender. The goal of this section is to put flesh and blood—individual voices—on these challenging labor conditions before delving into the standardized instrument introduced in part three.

About 30 unstructured phone or in-person interviews were conducted for this book with contingent and noncontingent faculty. Although not a representative sample, it represents a range of telling perspectives. When comments from these interviews are used, the names of interviewees are replaced with pseudonyms and their institutional affiliations are anonymized. In addition, to further minimize the risk to contingent faculty from potential retaliation for their comments, many of the comments used in the next chapters are taken from media accounts already in the public record as well as from the staff report by the House Committee on Education and the Democratic Staff (2014), which summarizes electronic forum responses to questions about the conditions of contingent faculty. It was administered in November and December of 2013 and includes responses from 845 contingent faculty members from 41 states.

4

Material Equity

Pay Parity, Job Security, and Benefits

Media reports abound on the difficulties faced by contingent faculty, who at certain institutions struggle to survive financially despite their advanced degrees and specialized knowledge. In addition to low pay and few (if any) benefits, contingent faculty often experience precarious employment, unsure if the job they have this semester will continue into the next, or even if the classes they've been assigned will be dropped at the last moment because of low enrollment. These uncertain work conditions can have distressing impacts on the finances and well-being of contingent faculty as well as negative ramifications for student outcomes.

This chapter takes a look at the three major challenges of material equity for non-tenure-track faculty: pay parity, job security, and benefits. The issues behind these three topics are discussed, and various comments from contingent faculty members give voice to the range of conditions they have encountered in their academic jobs.

Pay Parity Challenges

Pay parity for contingent faculty is a sensitive topic. After all, institutions began moving toward the use of contingent labor in the first place to save money. The CAW (2012) survey placed nationwide average contingent faculty pay at $2,235 per course at two-year colleges and $3,400 per course at four-year colleges and universities. The Adjunct Project, a crowd-sourced database of pay rates, lists the national average at $2,987 (June & Newman, 2013), with variations by state and discipline. For the sake of comparison to tenure-track faculty compensation, let's assume a full teaching load is 10 courses per year; using the higher number of $3,400 per course, that would result in annual pay of $34,000.

Contrast that amount with tenure-track faculty salaries. The *Chronicle of Education* almanac put nationwide average assistant professor pay among public two-year institutions at $54,101, and at four-year public institutions at $68,379 ("Data from the 2016 Almanac," 2016). According to a U.S. House committee staff report, "In order to garner comparable wages [to non-contingent faculty], an adjunct would have to teach nearly seventeen courses per year" (House Committee, 2014, p. 6). Of course, obtaining such a schedule is not only next to impossible, especially across institutions, but also an unmanageable workload.

Determining an optimal pay parity amount between contingent and tenure-track faculty is a contested issue. After all, equal pay for equal work does not mean advocates sometimes ignore the fact that contingent faculty are not asked to deliver as much departmental and institutional service (e.g., student advising, committee work, grant writing, or research publication) as tenure-track positions do. For example, a world-class researcher funded by major grants who leads a team of expert scientists on cancer research or sources of greener energy may justifiably earn $150,000 a year. In this case it is understandable that a half-time contingent faculty member teaching two or three classes a semester would not be paid $75,000 to meet an expectation of pay equity. But conversely, it is equally difficult to justify paying contingent faculty $3,400 for a class. So what ratio would be fair?

Some institutions do specifically articulate a parity definition, or the percentage of their tenure-track faculty members' workload that is covered by their teaching responsibilities alone. For example, Hanzimanolis (2013) found that 33 of 72 community college districts in California had explicitly defined work parity for part-time faculty. Work parity ranged from a low of 53% at West Hills Community College District to a high of 88% at Imperial, Sonoma, and Santa Barbara college districts. Although the mean was 76%, the median and mode were 75%, with 10 community college districts selecting that definition.

This book also adopts a 75% of assistant professor rate of pay as a straightforward parity definition for the standardized purposes of the Contingent Labor Conditions Score, assuming 10 semester-length courses per year as an equivalency to full time. Applying that 75% definition of pay parity to the nationwide averages of assistant professor compensation found in the 2016 *Chronicle of Education* almanac, two-year public institutions would pay on average just over $4,000 per course, and four-year public institutions would pay just over $5,100 per course ("Data from the 2016 Almanac," 2016). At these levels, contingent faculty would make an income ($40,000–$51,000) comparable to the beginning and middle tiers of compensation provided to our grade-school and high-school teachers, professions commonly understood as incredibly important to societal well-being, although modestly compensated. Instead, contingent faculty members are paid less than many service workers. Robin Sowards, an adjunct professor at Duquesne University in Pittsburgh, told reporters, "I have a colleague that works as [a] bartender, as well as an adjunct, and he makes far more money pouring beer than teaching" (Koma, 2014).

The cost of implementing higher pay for contingent faculty is high but modest compared to overall campus budgets. For instance, staying with the California Community Colleges example, the statewide California Community College Chancellor's Office (2017) reported 41,373 contingent faculty members in fall 2016. Imagine the cost if each person was each given $1,000 more per course, a rate that still would not fully close the equity gap. Nevertheless, if 40,000 contingent faculty members averaged a 2/2 teaching load, teaching 2 classes in the fall and 2 in the spring, (4 classes per year per instructor equals 165,492 classes total), then the raise would cost $165.5 million. To put these numbers in context, the raise would be just more than 1% of the total California Community Colleges' annual expenses, set at $14.64 billion according to the California Office of the Governor (Brown, 2017).

Although some fiscal conservatives may react against proposals to use more public funds to close pay-equity gaps, in this case, pay increases would likely save tax dollars. Taxpayers also suffer from the current treatment of contingent faculty, as revealed in the following:

> But these low incomes do pose taxpayer costs. According to analysis by the Congressional Research Service, a family of three in California relying solely on the median adjunct salary would qualify for, among other things, Medicaid, an earned income tax credit, a child tax credit, and food stamps, costing taxpayers $13,645 per year. (House Committee, 2014, p. 11)

Greater pay equity for contingent faculty would also require ongoing efforts because the cost of living and inflation often mount faster than pay increases. When asked if they receive regular salary increases, 79.2% of respondents to the CAW (2012) survey indicated that they do not. This means pay inequity is only growing year by year on most campuses.

The following comments in a report from the House Committee (2014) illustrate the kind of pain caused when salary levels for contingent faculty are far below what is required to live comfortably.

> My university pays $2,100 per class, which means even if I work at 100%, 10 classes per academic year, I would only make $21,000. (p. 5)

Growing up in a poor neighborhood . . . I believed earning several college degrees would be my path out of poverty—but that is no longer the case. (p. 7)

Because I was also the sole support of my two children . . . I relied on Medicaid to pay for the medical bills of my daughter. And, during the time I taught at the community college, I earned so little that I sold my plasma on Tuesdays and Thursdays to pay for her daycare costs. Seriously, my plasma paid for her daycare because I taught English as adjunct faculty. (p. 8)

I love what I do. I work incredible hours (my shortest work week is probably 50+ hours), and always through the weekends. I am lucky enough to have health insurance (which is over 1/10th of my total income), yet I probably make a tad over what someone on full benefits unemployment makes. I'll tell you straight—I make $28,000 before taxes. . . . My home life is a disaster—I never buy anything new, and often my bills are paid late or not at all. Think about what YOU could buy with less than $2,000 a month—it's not much, let me tell you, and we haven't even begun to discuss the nature of student loans. (p. 8)

While teaching . . . I found myself making so little money that I had to apply for food stamps and Medicaid to support myself, my wife, and our two young children (about ages 3 and 6 at the time). (p. 9)

In short, contingent faculty who do not have spouse or family support or other sources of income are often driven to public assistance programs. On top of this, job insecurity takes its toll even at institutions with higher-than-average pay per course. For example, one adjunct at Cabrillo College, one of the higher-paying community colleges, said, "Job insecurity takes years off of my life. Collecting unemployment is embarrassing and degrading and would be unnecessary with permanent employment and parity" (Took-Zozaya & Reynolds, 2013, p. 6). As challenging as the low pay is, the lack of permanence and resulting insecurity are often equally difficult to manage.

Job Security Challenges

As contract workers, contingent faculty do not have to be officially fired or laid off to find themselves without a job; they can simply not be reinvited to teach the following term. A measure of job security is an essential element for most workers in any profession. Unfortunately for contingent faculty, job security is often nonexistent.

As discussed in chapter 1, most contingent faculty do not view their teaching roles as a side job supplementing their primary income. Rather, most view their teaching as an essential component of their daily labor and a core component of their living wages (Coalition on the Academic Workforce, 2012). For this reason, a fair measure of job security is crucial. However, in academia, job security has historically been the gold standard form of tenure, which generally has had two purposes: to protect academic freedom in research and teaching and to create financial security that will attract talented individuals. These two basic principles established in 1925 were reaffirmed in 1940 by the AAUP and the Association of American Colleges & Universities (Association of American University Professors, n.d). It has been continually reaffirmed and subsequently endorsed by more than 200 academic institutions, including leading education associations (e.g., the NEA and the Association for the Study of Higher Education) and discipline-specific national associations (e.g., American Sociological Association, American Psychological Association, American Political Science Association, Modern Language Association).

Tenure has long been held as the ideal compensation plan in academia; however, it is not the only method of protecting academic freedom (discussed in chapter 5) or providing sufficient financial security to attract talent. In terms of job security, some higher education administrators have been reluctant to seek middle-path options. For example, the University of California system has what it calls a lecturer with potential security of employment. A person in this position, after a designated number of years of positive service can move to a lecturer, also with security of employment, and even eventually get another promotion to senior lecturer with security of employment. Although the positions pay less than tenured faculty, they are usually full-time and considerably better than working on a term-to-term contract basis. Yet, positions like these are rare (even within the University of California system just mentioned). Fiscally, using contingent faculty without job security or protections is a much cheaper alternative to tenure-line hiring. Middle routes would not provide savings as large as those gained from using contingent faculty. Politically, faculty members have largely resisted new forms of reimagining the professoriate. Thus, rather than create a graduated set of variously compensated faculty types, a two-tiered hierarchy began to emerge in which the tenure and contingent lines have grown increasingly farther apart.

A statement must be made here on what the goal of tenure is not. The purpose of an academic institution is not to provide faculty with guaranteed lifetime employment without accountability or work-quality expectations. Fair evaluations agreed on by faculty representatives and administrators are commendable. Tenure has its limits, and a tenured employee can be fired for several reasons depending on the contracts at each institution. Tenure-track positions have always been more difficult for faculty to land than contingent appointments and have typically required a competitive national job search.

Further, the duration of time before an assistant professor is up for tenure review is historically six or seven years, and a successful tenure bid is dependent on a significant number of refereed publications, the number and quality of grants won, and often other teaching or service responsibilities. In fact, one report looking at 10 leading research universities noted that only 53% of assistant professors achieved tenure (Dooris & Guidos, 2006).

Many options exist between a full tenure system and a completely insecure contingent employment system. In terms of job security, this has to do with features such as rehire rights, priority of assignment, seniority systems, multiyear contracts, a grievance process to redress violations, and so forth.

Again, the following comments in the House Committee (2014) report are illuminating.

> Job stability: None. As adjuncts, we never know if we will be rehired from semester to semester. The process for hire or rehire has no transparency. Classes for adjuncts are assigned or cancelled less than a week before the semester begins, every semester. (p. 21)

> No insurance, no unemployment insurance, [and no] assurance that I will have a job next semester. . . . It's December 7th. I still don't know if they will have classes for me at the beginning of January. (p. 21)

> In all cases I was not told I would not be working for them the next quarter. I simply had to wait and see, and in all cases I was not offered another class. I taught four course[s] in the fall, but was not told until the day before spring semester started that I wouldn't have any classes for the spring. I was unemployed with no notice. (p. 21–22)

Working conditions like these make planning for the future nearly impossible. Contingent faculty members do not know how many courses they will teach the next term, if they will be teaching at all—let alone with no say in the courses selected, their times, or locations. Parallel to a kind of Maslovian hierarchy of needs, focusing on high-level functions like pedagogical excellence is more difficult when lower-level needs like basic job and wage stability go unmet. The good news is that basic policies, such as rehire rights, are relatively straightforward to implement and can significantly improve job security for contingent faculty.

Rehire Rights

Rehire rights are by far the most important component of job security. Some campuses provide rehire rights for contingent faculty, although they differ widely and tend to be on the weaker side at most community colleges.

According to the CAW (2012) survey, when asked if any form of job security exists based on seniority or time of service, 19.4% of faculty with a union said yes; where no union existed, a paltry 3.9% said yes. Most unions have worked to create contractual language around this, although in many places the written policies are regularly challenged and often go unenforced. At a minimum level, partial job security is in order. This may take the form of an explicitly written understanding that course assignments will go to current contingent faculty before new faculty are hired. Without such an agreement, many contingent faculty members are unable to psychologically invest in an institution. Rehire rights may fairly be tied to performance or evaluations before they are granted to a contingent faculty member.

Consistency of Assignment

This is particularly important for the freeway flyers, contingent faculty teaching at multiple institutions or who have other day jobs that are not on a flexible schedule. If contingent faculty members are suddenly assigned courses on different days or times for an upcoming semester, it can conflict with their other responsibilities. Further, some campuses do not allow an instructor to turn down offered courses and still keep his or her seniority. This is especially problematic when an instructor is asked to take on multiple new courses he or she has not previously taught. When this happens, the work and time spent in preparation for a new course are considerably greater. Although many teachers enjoy new courses from time to time for the challenge and change, some form of basic security is laudable so that contingent faculty members are not forced to teach outside their areas of expertise just to avoid forfeiting rehire rights.

In an interview with Elaine, a community college adjunct professor in San Diego, she tells a story about how her seniority disappeared when she had to decline a last-minute request for courses the following term that conflicted with courses she was already scheduled to teach at another campus.

> There was no alert or warning. I only found out later when I asked if I had achieved priority of assignment. It turns out I had lost it because I had turned down the offer. But it wasn't even a fair offer, or at a time I had previously taught.

A final point to mention regarding consistency of assignment is the practice at many institutions of giving tenure-track faculty preference on assignments over long-term contingent faculty. The practice may be understandable in general, but it can become exploitative when it is still allowed after contingent faculty contracts have already been offered or when it is done for the purpose of giving tenure-track faculty overtime assignments to supplement their income. If tenure-track faculty get first selection of courses before long-term contingent faculty, then they should at least wait to select overtime courses until long-term contingent faculty have been given contracts.

Breaks in Service

Most workers, especially contingent workers with multiple part-time jobs, may have competing priorities or life challenges that require them to decline an assignment for a term here or there. Perhaps it is the birth of a child, a severe illness, a schedule change at another institution, or any number of other personal or professional reasons that leads to the break. When institutions show very little commitment to their contingent faculty members, the practice of replacing those same contingent faculty the moment they show less than a full commitment to the institution is particularly cruel. Many institutions have some form of policy or contract language concerning this, such as allowing a semester off every two or three years without surrendering seniority or contract status. In institutions where rehire rights require multiple years of service, accrual of time should not be wiped out after simply declining an assignment for one term on a rare occasion.

Cancellation Compensation

For employees cobbling a piecemeal wage together from multiple teaching contracts, the sudden loss of a contract can be a devastating blow to their financial security. Consider the hardship placed on contingent faculty members when they decline a course at another institution or rearrange their family or work obligations to teach a course offered to them only to find that because of low enrollment, they are suddenly without the class and it is too late to find another assignment. The institution should offer some compensation for the hardship. The CAW (2012) survey found that at unionized campuses, 17.9% said there was compensation for cancellations, contrasted with 9.9% at nonunionized campuses.

There is always the chance that the department will find itself with suddenly fewer classes to offer as a result of reduced enrollments. Full-time faculty members are typically protected from this because contingent faculty members are hired to be the flexible workforce. As one contingent faculty member said:

> I am an excellent and well-credentialed teacher in good standing in the department, but I was told that next quarter instead of the twenty credits I thought I was going to teach, I will only get ten—a $6,000 pay cut. (House Committee, 2014, p. 22)

Rodney, a tenured community college professor in Northern California who participates in scheduling, was interviewed about his feelings on the situation and displayed a kind of reluctantly accepting attitude.

> I understand it's not ideal for a lot of people. But, we don't do it for no reason. We can't predict enrollments. Every market and every industry has fluctuations, and we have a fiscal obligation to avoid overstaffing with permanent faculty. Most of us [full-timers] have been in their [contingent] shoes; I was a part-timer for five years. I remember waiting to see what would be given to me. Luckily for part-time instructors here, the longer-term ones have rights over newer ones, as well as before full-time faculty can take overload assignments.

Rodney is referring to the policy at some campuses in which full-time faculty are not allowed to ask for additional courses for overtime pay beyond their standard full-time assignment until certain longer-serving groups of adjuncts have been given their offerings. This policy prevents some of the most capricious instances of contingent faculty losing a course at the last minute.

Grievance Process

Despite the best of intentions and even the most explicitly written contracts or agreements, violations will inevitably occur. When an employee's rights are violated or the employee perceives that a violation has occurred, a process to address the matter should exist. The worst campuses have few channels for redress, leave the process vague, and require individual contingent faculty to approach administrators directly about their concerns. A much better work environment is when contingent faculty have clearly written agreements and a point of contact selected by the faculty or the faculty union serving as a consultant and advocate to help individual faculty members address their concerns. If this point of contact is the department chair, dean, someone in human resources, or another administrator, the fear of retaliation can create a chilling effect. Thus the point of contact should be a faculty or union representative who facilitates interaction with human resources and the administration.

Benefits Challenges

As contingent faculty at the most inequitable campuses know, meager pay and job insecurity are not the only ills they suffer; benefits are typically nonexistent as well, as the following House Committee (2014) comments illustrate:

I am "permitted" to join the health insurance plan, as long as I pay 100% of the premium. (p. 17)

As far as benefits go, we have a sham "retirement" plan. . . . It is a contribution to COBRA [the Consolidated Omnibus Budget Reconciliation Act of 1985] where there is NO employer match. . . . We also have NO health insurance help. (p. 17)

Teaching two courses per semester—assuming my upcoming Spring classes won't be cancelled or reassigned—I'll earn $8,000 this year. That is not a typo. This is well below the federal poverty level for an individual. I now qualify for Medicaid under the Affordable Care Act in my state . . . and I have already applied for coverage. (p. 7)

Next, benefits are examined in more depth in three categories: health, retirement, and other types.

Health

According to an AFT (2010) survey, contingent faculty received health insurance at 42% of four-year public campuses, 28% of four-year private campuses, and 16% of two-year campuses. Of the contingent faculty respondents to the CAW (2012) survey, only 4.3% received health benefits that are paid in full by their academic employer, 14.6% received health benefits with costs split between employee and employer, and another 3.6% received a health plan through their academic employer with the entire cost falling on the employee.

The Patient Protection and Affordable Care Act (2010) brought some changes. The act was upheld by the Supreme Court against challenges in 2012 and implemented in 2014 with enforcement beginning in 2016. Although the plan is intended to make health care more affordable and widespread, it has had mixed consequences for adjuncts. On the positive side, the act has a gradation of subsidies for those who fall below the federal marker of 400% of the poverty rate. For a single person, the poverty rate was set at $11,670 in 2014 (U.S. Department of Health & Human Services, 2014). Almost no contingent faculty members make four times that amount, or $46,680. The following comments illustrate how the Affordable Care Act has helped some contingent faculty:

Two and a half years ago I let my health insurance go. I needed to choose between paying rent, maintaining a commuter car and health insurance. Under the Affordable Care Act, I now qualify for a $398 subsidy and I have signed up through coveredca.com. (House Committee, 2014, p. 17)

My wife and I are currently uninsured, and are very grateful finally to be able to get insurance through the Affordable Care Act. (House Committee, 2014, p. 17)

The Patient Protection and Affordable Care Act (2010) mandates that all employers with 50 or more employees, virtually all colleges, provide health insurance for their full-time employees or face penalties (*full-time* is defined as those who work 30 hours per week or more). Although Affordable Care Act policies may change depending on efforts by the Trump administration, so far the 30-hour definition has led many campuses to cap contingent hours below that number (e.g., Flaherty, 2012b), forcing more contingent faculty into multi-institution freeway-flyer situations, adding additional stress and cost to an already overburdened workforce. This is conveyed by the following comments from contingent faculty:

I was supposed to teach three courses this fall, but the university cancelled one of my courses in August, the week before the semester started. The reason was to avoid having to give me any benefits, including health care, due to the Affordable Care Act. (House Committee, 2014, p. 18)

Part-time lecturers at my university do not have the option of employer-provided health insurance, and the university plans to reduce workload opportunities even further for individual part-time lecturers in the year to come in order to avoid negative consequences [to the university] of the Affordable Care Act. Because of this, most of my colleagues and I work multiple jobs. (House Committee, 2014, p. 18)

There's frustration and anger and sadness and resentment, you know, but you don't have a voice. But it's going to be a silent type of thing, because we're the most vulnerable part of campus life. It's not like we can dial up our [American Federation of Teachers] rep and say, "Hey, we're getting the short end of the stick here." (Flaherty, 2012a, para. 8)

If faculty members do buy into campus or state health plans, they still may lack other typical perks for full-time faculty, as shown in the following comments:

We do not have paid vacation, sick or personal days. If I am sick, I cannot cancel class without potential reprisal from the administration. . . . Retirement benefits for me take quadruple the time to accrue as they do for a full-time professor. Unemployment compensation is denied us. (House Committee, 2014, p. 19)

I am currently pregnant with my first child. . . . I will receive NO time off for the birth or recovery. It is necessary I continue until the end of the semester in May in order to get paid, something I drastically need. (House Committee, 2014, p. 19)

Retirement

According to the CAW (2012) survey, 5.3% of contingent faculty receive retirement benefits paid in full by their academic employer; 26.9% receive retirement benefits with split costs between employee and employer; and 9.2% receive a retirement plan through their academic employer, but the entire cost is on the employee. One contingent faculty member commented, "I don't earn enough to save for retirement. Every month is a struggle to just pay the basic bills. My 'retirement' plan is to work until they bury me" (House Committee, 2014, p. 16).

Other Benefits

Many forms of benefits exist beyond the basics of health and retirement. According to the AFT (2010) survey, 9% of contingent faculty members receive paid vacation, 17% receive paid personal leave, and 29% receive paid sick leave. Other benefits that can be found in professional jobs but are rare for contingent faculty members include items like subsidized life insurance, tuition, childcare, meal plans, gym or recreation plans, transportation, or housing allowances. Such benefits indicate the value of employees and help retain talent. At the same time, many industries forgo these types of boosts for employees. Although these are nice and encouraged, the most important are the health and retirement benefits that have long been part of the general social contract to laboring Americans.

When it comes to job benefits in general for contingent faculty, college administrators have difficult decisions to make that

> require striking a balance between the two fundamental obligations of every governing board: 1) the fiduciary responsibility to control costs, and 2) the strategic responsibility to ensure the health and well-being of faculty and staff, on whom the vitality of the entire institution depends. (Kirch, 2013)

A Note About Unionization

Unions can be helpful for contingent faculty and divisive for the campus. For example, consider the 23-campus California State University system, which has one of the strongest faculty unions in the country. The union has an organized presence across each campus, particularly in contract negotiation years. In spring 2016 the faculty threatened the administration with a systemwide strike and won pay raises across all tiers of faculty. Again, this presents a situation that is beneficial to contingent faculty's compensation structure yet creates stress and contention on campus.

The California State University system also has full-time instructors who are not on the tenure track and do not have research responsibilities but do have reasonable job security and a livable wage. Although full-time instructors are not used en masse, the few who are employed earn $56,781 on average, which has much greater pay parity to an assistant professor, who makes $73,919 on average (California State University, 2016).

Nonetheless, earning and maintaining equitable pay has not been easy at some California State University campuses. One interviewee, Jane, who had worked with the California Faculty Association (CFA) at California State University, Long Beach revealed some of the intense efforts the CFA had to regularly make to protect contingents' rights. In the CFA contract, a temporary faculty employee who teaches for six years begins to receive three-year contracts. She recounts a specific time the CFA had to get involved to uphold the integrity of those contracts.

> So this one department was laying people off right before they would get their three-year contracts. Not because there was no work, because then they gave the courses to other people. So two lecturers came to us who had been laid off, and we were like, "They cannot do this!" So we took that fight to [the administration] and it went to arbitration, and we won! They got their three-year contracts and back pay for the classes they should have been given. It sent a message, because till then the departments were always trying to do sneaky stuff like that, so we really had to keep an eye out to make sure contingent faculty rights were being protected.

Although this situation had a positive outcome, it reveals the unfortunate reality that most gains for contingent faculty are neither won nor maintained without ongoing vigilance and effort to defend their working conditions. As Cynthia, a contingent faculty member and union representative at a community college in the San Diego area said in an e-mail to other adjuncts,

> Just because something is in our contract does not mean it will go unchallenged. You have to be ready to stand your ground and file grievances when your rights are being threatened. If you just go with the flow, they will take what they can get. A contract means nothing if it is not enforced. It is only enforced if *we* enforce it. (Cynthia, personal communication, May 2014)

Unionization has historically allowed American workers to make a living wage and achieve fair labor conditions. Of course, unions are not without their critics and political ramifications. Although this book does not advocate for or against unionization per se, it should be noted that it is always better when faculty are given fair pay and benefits for work produced without having to actively fight for wages or challenge administrators.

What an A Grade for Material Equity Looks Like

The North American leader of egalitarian practices for contingent faculty comes from Canada. The Vancouver Community College (VCC) system has achieved pay equity for part-time faculty, job security based on seniority, and a highly transparent system including published lists of seniority rankings (Cosco & Longmate, 2012). Within a year of teaching, contingent (called *term* at VCC) faculty members automatically become regular faculty. There is only one pay scale for all faculty, so if someone works 50% of the load of a full-time person then he or she gets 50% of the rate of pay of a full-time worker. There is no two-tier system, and all have the opportunity to become full-time via seniority. VCC's model was built after decades of negotiations and collective bargaining. It illustrates what is possible when faculty work together and organize in a democratic process for change. Frank Cosco, president of the VCC Faculty Association, said, "Once you're hired as a term instructor, people take it very seriously because the department heads and deans know that this person is going to be around awhile" (June, 2010, para. 2).

As the dean of the college's music school, who started as a part-time faculty member, said,

> A lot of people who work part time for us are grounded in this institution and continue to develop themselves professionally. They have a particular affinity for this institution. The likelihood of them leaving this position is not very high. (June, 2010, para. 17)

Further, benefits are a reality for contingent faculty at some of the most equitable institutions in the United States:

> I am paid much more than most adjunct faculty, and I have the same benefits as tenured faculty—medical, dental, vision, retirement. (House Committee, 2014, p. 30)

> For now, due primarily to our faculty union, I make a decent salary, have full health benefits, and am looking forward to retiring with a modest pension. I work at [school] which is a better place than most for adjuncts

thanks to a union contract that gives us access to health insurance and a minimal number of paid sick days. (House Committee, 2014, p. 30)

Thus, contingency does not have to be a marker of exploitation, and straightforward steps can be taken to move toward an empowered and fairly compensated teaching force. Although pay parity remains elusive for many contingent faculty members in the United States, pockets of equity are springing up that provide hope and a vision for change.

5

Professional Equity

Opportunities for Development and Advancement

Where chapter 4 deals more with economic and material conditions for contingent faculty, this chapter focuses on issues of social psychology and organizational culture. A campus supportive of contingent faculty members' identity as professionals will reap dividends in employee morale and productivity. High faculty satisfaction is a win for not only faculty but also students, whose learning conditions are linked to faculty morale and investment.

One of the most difficult conditions facing contingent faculty, beyond material conditions, is the deleterious nature that precarious employment has on the psyche, key social relationships, and the general well-being of the worker (e.g., Feldman, 1996; Kalleberg, 2011). Dissatisfaction is particularly acute for those who would not voluntarily choose a contingent or part-time position if noncontingent positions were available (Maynard & Joseph, 2008). Further, few contingent faculty had visions of downwardly mobile careers while they were pursuing the advanced degrees required for their positions.

It is true that teaching at the college level is widely held as fulfilling and intellectually stimulating work, and it comes with some measure of social status as well. It is also true that a large portion of contingent faculty indicate they do not teach primarily for the paycheck, but this can be misleading. For example, in a survey of contingent faculty by the American Federation of Teachers (2010), 57% of respondents stated that their salaries are falling short; the same percentage (57%) said they do their jobs primarily because they like teaching, and it was not for the money. Just focusing on the happy-to-teach-despite-the-money side would give the wrong impression. Most contingent faculty are concerned with their low pay. After all, it would make little sense to respond that you do a job primarily for the money when the money is so meager. As Maynard and Joseph (2008) found, the contingent faculty who prefer part-time positions have higher job satisfaction than those who prefer full-time positions. The study by the American Federation of Teachers (2010) also found that contingent faculty members felt that

- it is important to establish more full-time positions at their institutions (68%),
- the number of such positions has stagnated or is decreasing (70%), and
- they are not given a fair opportunity for consideration when a full-time position becomes available (44%).

The individual choices of contingent faculty are not independent of the institution's organizational features. The interplay between campus organizational cultures and structures on students' experiences, choices, and outcomes has been documented by sociologists of higher education (Armstrong & Hamilton, 2013; Binder & Wood, 2013; Stevens, 2007); the same mechanisms work on faculty as well.

To discuss professional equity more specifically, it is useful to divide it into two categories—opportunity and identity. Professional opportunity looks at ladders of professional development that exist in the organization, whereas professional identity examines how contingent faculty members perceive the institution in relation to their careers. Thus, professional opportunity (e.g., on-the-job training or rungs for promotion) focuses on the objective structures that exist on campus for contingent faculty, whereas professional identity examines the subjective campus culture (e.g., experiences of inclusion versus exclusion in the department) experienced by contingent faculty. The following topics and subtopics are also the components of the professional equity grade on the Contingent Labor Conditions Score outlined in chapter 7.

- Professional opportunity for contingent faculty
  - o Professional development
  - o Opportunity for advancement
  - o Academic freedom
- Professional identity of contingent faculty
  - o Contingent faculty's inclusion
  - o Contingent faculty's satisfaction

Professional Opportunity for Contingent Faculty

Professional Development

Development can come in a variety of formats. Four of the most basic are used in the Contingent Labor Conditions Score introduced in part three of this book. Considerations around professional development for contingent faculty include the following:

- Does the campus have an orientation program for new contingent faculty?
- Does the campus have workshops and support for learning new technology or pedagogical techniques?
- Does the campus supply the faculty with funds to participate in conferences and join professional associations?
- Do contingent faculty get to participate in the shared governance of the campus and department?

Orientations for new contingent faculty are incredibly helpful, yet not consistently practiced. They should include at least a basic introduction to the campus and department. On some campuses, contingent faculty get their introduction only by asking questions, such as where and how to get a parking pass, a campus e-mail account, an ID card, and library and work room access. Better orientations cover these practical needs and also include introductions to other staff and faculty across the campus.

Many campuses have centers for teaching excellence, but access to these resources and workshops is often unevenly distributed to contingent faculty. Contingent faculty should be granted access to these helpful resources; it would also be appropriate to compensate them for their time, especially when the training has to do with topics like learning a campus's specific online teaching platform (e.g., Moodle, Canvas, or BlackBoard) or in-class media carts.

Staying current in one's field requires interaction with other professionals and their research. Tenure-track faculty members are often granted a certain amount of funding to cover professional association memberships or conference travel. Some form of similar funding, even if proportionately smaller, goes a long way in signaling campus support of contingent faculty members' professional development.

A seat at the table of shared governance has multiple potential impacts for contingent faculty members, especially if key decisions can be made about compensation or job security. Thus, faculty governance is also linked to material equity. Policy outcomes of such roles are important, and, in addition, the very act of participation in steering the direction of the institution is a profound source of professional development. The faculty member gains experience in the inner workings of the campus, the political environment, and knowing who the key players are in a particular setting while gaining confidence in his or her efficacy to influence change.

Opportunity for Advancement

When a new teaching-oriented position opens up, are senior contingent faculty on campus who have served consistently with positive evaluations considered for the position or at least given the opportunity to interview? This is one area particularly germane to institutions that do not evaluate faculty based on research skill. If the primary responsibility of the role is to teach, a track record of positive service at the institution should be sufficient to indicate the ability of the faculty member. At institutions where a small portion of the role is based on a research agenda, like comprehensive four-year liberal arts colleges, then seniority as an adjunct should at least count toward the opportunity to be seriously considered and interviewed along with outside applicants. For research-oriented faculty positions, prioritizing internal candidates based on teaching seniority may not make quite as much sense.

Adrianna Kezar (2013) identifies four departmental culture types across campuses based on how they treat their non-tenure-track faculty (destructive, neutral, inclusive, and learning) and the impact such treatment has on their performance. Although her constructs are not exactly parallel with the Contingent Labor Conditions Score grades on professional equity, they examine related underlying concepts. Therefore, Kezar's article is recommended reading in tandem with this chapter.

Professional opportunities are sharply limited at the most exploitative campuses. Kezar (2013) offers the following description of destructive cultures for contingent faculty:

> The departments tend to be elitist in perspective, believing only faculty who have earned a doctorate, obtained a tenure-track position, and are awarded tenure are worthy academics. The department chair and most of the tenure-track faculty within departments that have this culture do not feel that NTTF [non-tenure-track faculty] are qualified instructors or professionals. As a result of the feelings of disrespect, NTTF typically are not listed as faculty in departmental materials, never mentioned as part of faculty, have low pay, and [do not] have any institutional protections or safeguards ignored by the chair (such as allowing them participation in meetings, orientation, benefits, or market-rate pay). (p. 164)

In such situations, even decades of dedicated teaching with strong evaluations may not lead to promotions, raises, or even consideration for permanent opportunities when they arise. Adjuncts in these types of situations made the following comments in the report from the House Committee, 2014):

> It is very common for an experienced adjunct to be passed over for a position, and it is given to a brand new graduate. (p. 23)

> I cannot earn a living working in higher education, regardless of my credentials and over 20 years of teaching experience. (p. 15)

It is impossible for adjuncts to earn a decent living and impossible to have any career advancement. We are shut out of regular teaching jobs and are shut out of full time employment by our own schools. (p. 23)

One adjunct asked [the administrator] if she would give preference in hiring to adjuncts. She replied, "Not only will I not give preference to adjuncts, I want people who have been out in the world doing things, not teaching." This was the impetus for us to form a union. We realized the futures for which we had prepared would be denied to us unless we worked together to change our situation. (p. 30)

Scholarly efforts have been made to reframe scholarship and faculty reward structures to value teaching more (e.g., Boyer, 1990; Braxton, Luckey, & Helland, 2002; O'Meara & Rice, 2005), yet most four-year campuses continue to hold refereed research publications as the gold standard of work performance. This may make sense at research universities, but for the thousands of other institutions, the majority of faculty members are tasked with the primary role of teaching. At these institutions, bringing seniority and experience into the hiring equation makes sense. Yet, faculty often like to imitate up and copy features of higher-ranked universities rather than imitate down and embrace policies used at, for example, K–12 public schools.

No opportunity for advancement means that many adjuncts are in dead-end roles. Others hold out hope for full-time positions, but such jobs are scarce on campuses with an overreliance on contingent labor, as illustrated in these comments from the House Committee (2014) report.

At [my school] 82% of faculty are "part-time" and the trend is only getting worse. (p. 4)

There are really no opportunities for advancement because there [are] very few full-time opportunities available, most likely because the schools are using more and more adjunct instructors instead of adding the higher-paid full-time positions. (p. 4)

My hope is that once I receive the degree I will get a full-time position, but I realize that this may not happen as universities continue to cut faculty positions and pay and move to using more adjunct instructors. (p. 4)

Some argue that institutions, out of a need for a core faculty to run departments, cannot possibly keep the increasing contingent trend going; however, certain for-profit schools have taken this strategy to great extremes. It is not uncommon to find all-administrative campuses whose faculty pool is made up almost entirely of part-time adjuncts under the direction of various staff administrators. Although such institutions may have increased access to college for some students, they face a host of difficulties like disturbingly low graduation rates, high student loan default rates, questionable educational quality, degrees devalued by employers, and more.

When a college education has been stripped down to piecework for independent contractors who have other full-time jobs, it becomes a very different commodity from an education delivered by lifetime committed professional educators. As one contingent faculty member said,

> When you pay an adjunct only for the contact hours they spend in the classroom, it doesn't give adjuncts a lot of motivation to spend extra time. . . . I have heard some adjuncts say, "I'm not going to put in all this extra time, because they don't think we're worth paying us other than our time in class." Many of us put in the time anyway, because we love teaching and helping our students succeed, but the system certainly doesn't reward it. I caution my students about choosing education as a career path. I would not wish their lives to turn out like mine has. (House Committee, 2014, p. 27)

This sense of not wishing this life on one's students points to the low pay and low optimism of contingent faculty stuck in dead-end jobs that do not offer chances for professional or financial advancement.

Academic Freedom

Chapter 4 raised the topic of tenure and its core purposes. Tenure has long been considered the idealized model for providing job security and academic freedom. However, this book also explores avenues for increasing both of those needs separately from tenure. To a research scholar, academic freedom is the ability to pursue unpopular, risky, or politically controversial research agendas without fear of reprisal. The correlate to teaching scholars has to do with the degree to which faculty are free to teach controversial material, challenge students' ideas to expand their capacity for critical thinking, and grade rigorously without fear of student complaints leading to their contract not being renewed. When such complaints inevitably do arise, do contingent faculty feel there is a supportive structure for them to voice their side of the story and to appeal or file grievances if they believe they are subject to retaliation?

The teacher scholar also considers academic freedom to involve a professional educator's sovereignty to select his or her own pedagogical techniques and practices. The opposite is when a predesigned course is handed down to a teacher to merely facilitate. Optional materials are one thing, and are often appreciated, especially by new contingent faculty or when teaching a new course. The challenge to academic freedom is when standardized materials are required. The question here is, to what degree has the curriculum been standardized and mandated to include prefabricated syllabi, course materials, assignments, and assessments?

In situations where specific course materials are mandated, faculty often feel as if they are viewed as incapable of developing their own courses. Some campuses create large swaths of course offerings based on standardized models. This typically happens with introductory courses (which are most of the offerings at community colleges) and online courses where the course template includes assignments and materials embedded in the course management software. An interviewee for this book, Alexander, said the following about his experience at a suburban community college:

> They want all the core classes standardized, mainly because they use so many adjuncts that they can't maintain evaluations of teaching quality. So instead of spending time making sure they have quality people they can trust, they just make us all follow the course guides the tenured faculty put together. It doesn't matter that I've taught this class at another institution a dozen times with my own course design. There is no sense of individuality; to them, all adjuncts are the same necessary problems to be managed.

Building a professional identity is difficult when the work is increasingly routinized and simplified into a merely facilitative role. Controversial topics and ideas that challenge the status quo are also often lost when curricula are standardized.

Professional Identity

Limits for professional development and advancement are not the only detrimental impacts on contingent educators; exploitative working conditions also erode contingent faculty members' sense of professional identity. The worst campuses subject their faculty to degrading situations that make them feel excluded, embarrassed, and often alienated from their labor and the intellectual life of the institution, as illustrated in the following comments from the House Committee (2014) report:

> To make ends meet, besides teaching at the community college, I also deliver pizzas. I feel that I lose the respect of my students when they see me delivering pizzas! (p. 15)

I hold my obligatory "office hours" in a bustling copy room. (p. 10)

Opportunities for growth and advancement, job stability, and administrative and professional support—they are all structured in a framework that sees contingent faculty not as faculty [but] more like contractors and performing unimportant labor. (p. 23)

These conditions make it impossible to dedicate my full attention to the success of my students because I spend almost as much time driving from institution(s) and looking for jobs elsewhere as I do prepping lectures, grading assignments, developing curriculum, etc. (p. 27)

The contingent faculty members who find themselves in these types of situations have hard decisions to make. They can compromise their professional ethics as teachers and overload their schedules to make ends meet, which often requires cutting corners on class prep and grading standards. This may lead to watering down the education they provide and affecting student learning as a result. Or contingent faculty can do what often amounts to volunteer labor on top of very low pay. They are stuck between professional compromise and professional martyrdom. One adjunct despairingly wrote:

We feel disposable, . . . a kind of "mark of Cain" between adjunct faculty and full-time faculty. . . . When the system you work under devalues your labor in the manner it does, for as long as it has, you can't help but begin to believe you are worthless. *I am a fraud, a fake*, I have felt, have told myself countless times. (Van Duyne, 2014, para. 24)

The lost sense of professionalism is alienating and isolating. Scott Langston, an adjunct at Texas Christian University, summarized the feeling.

There always remains a certain stigma to my adjuncting . . . failure, second-rate, loser, embarrassment. After all, it was not my career goal to be an adjunct. This feeling can be especially strong when dealing with administrators and full-time faculty. I often feel like a stray dog, roaming from institution to institution, getting a scrap—a class or two—here and there, even a pat on the head, but not really being fully embraced as a part of any place. I suppose that is one of the most difficult things about adjuncting, not being a part of any community, or at least not feeling like a part. (Langston, 2006, para. 4)

Professional identity emerges from the interplay among an individual, his or her field, and his or her organization of employment. What contingent faculty members think about the campus and its influence on their careers is consequential. Similarly, do contingent faculty members feel respected at their institution and by their noncontingent colleagues? Professional identity is measured in the Contingent Labor Conditions Score (see chapter 7) in terms of contingent faculty members' experiences of inclusion and satisfaction.

Contingent Faculty's Inclusion

What proportion of contingent faculty feel like they really are members of the department and campus community? Examples of organizational inclusion are designated office space, a Web biography, and invitations to faculty meetings and events. These gestures offer a sense of presence, if not permanence, that go a long way toward signaling a sense of membership. Are contingent faculty treated with a basic level of collegiality and inclusion, or are they left with feelings of anonymity?

Social inclusion matters in personal and professional arenas. Sociologist Peter Marsden (2000) writes about how our social networks provide emotional support and shape our very identities. Unfortunately, contingent faculty members are often isolated from one another and lose out on the advantage of forming and maintaining networks with other colleagues. As one contingent faculty member put it, "As an adjunct, you're very isolated. You're on campus briefly, then you're running off crosstown to another campus. You don't get to make those sort of water cooler connections" (Schackner, 2013).

If a contingent faculty member is planning to make a long-term career out of his or her teaching commitment to the campus, a sense of belonging to the scholarly community and life of the department is necessary. Unfortunately, this is not terribly common, as an adjunct instructor illustrates in the following:

> Although I've been at my present Very Decent University job for the past 15 years, a tenured professor asked me, "So, you're teaching for US this semester?" Why am I not part of this "us" after so much dedicated teaching, year after year? (House Committee, 2014, p. 23)

Kezar (2013) writes that when campuses are indeed inclusive of contingent faculty they contain the following traits:

> [Contingent faculty] were likely to be respected and treated as colleagues. This respect translated into being invited to all meetings and events and actively being brought into governance, including curricular decisions. Not

only were NTTF [non-tenure-track faculty] brought into departmental governance, but they were also more likely to be encouraged to participate in campus-wide service. (p. 172)

Contingent Faculty's Satisfaction

Industrial organizational psychologists have long known that satisfaction and morale are key components of employee engagement and productivity. As described in more detail in chapters 7 and 8, the Contingent Labor Conditions Score measures job satisfaction in the following areas: compensation, departmental support, experiences of collegiality, and academic freedom. When contingent faculty begin to lose their energy and enthusiasm for teaching in the face of poor pay, heavy workloads, and lack of professional respect, their job performance may decline. This can have adverse effects on student learning outcomes and experiences. One contingent instructor observed:

> I am still relatively new to and excited about the experience of teaching. The lack of support I receive from the university is wearing me down though. I can sense in myself the inclination to "go through the motions" of my job. (House Committee, 2014, p. 24)

This inclination to go through the motions is compounded by insufficient time to offer out-of-class support to students.

> I am limited in the amount of time I can spend at my office, having office hours, and otherwise serving my institution and my career, since I am not paid enough to afford childcare beyond the hours that I spend teaching. (House Committee, 2014, p. 27)

As contingent faculty teach the same courses multiple times, there is a growing temptation to simplify the workflow as much as possible to take on additional courses. This can lead to a situation where contingent faculty have hundreds of students per term across their courses. With so many students, faculty members generally stop attempting to remember names, grade essays, or help students outside class times. Always scrambling for more courses, especially online and across institutions, is an unfortunate survival strategy that does not serve students well.

Interestingly, campuses with large numbers of voluntary contingent faculty members tend to have higher morale and job satisfaction. Those who choose part-time work for its flexibility are able to teach without creating more competition for the occasional full-time jobs that become available.

Cindy, an adjunct at a small religiously affiliated college in Orange County, CA, stated:

> I am a part-time professor because I want to write and I hate meetings. But I have no idea how people do it [working part-time] that are trying to support a family on it. I may eventually want to be full-time, but because of my spouse's job I don't have to worry about that now.

Although Cindy's satisfaction and external sources of security are nice, her comments reveal an ill-fated trend in higher education, which is that teaching is a luxury profession for those who are supported by a spouse or are financially secure. This creates class barriers for others trying to make a living wage.

What an A Grade in Professional Equity Looks Like

Contingent faculty at A institutions (according to the Contingent Labor Conditions Score in chapter 7) feel strongly that they are a welcome part of the professional and learning communities. They are given the same, or at least very similar, opportunities for growth and advancement as their full-time counterparts, with a clear promotional process. Their access to professional development includes conference and professional memberships and, in some cases, money for special projects or contingent-led initiatives and ideas. When a permanent position becomes available, existing faculty feel they have a serious shot at the job if their evaluations have been strong. Contingent faculty at A institutions feel like full members of decision-making groups and hold a respected place in the academic community. With some variation, contingent faculty are likely to be quite satisfied with most areas of their jobs. In turn, these engaged contingent faculty members create an ideal setting for student learning to take place. Kezar (2013) writes of such cultures, noting that

> faculty, chairs, and staff in the learning culture typically thought about support for NTTF [non-tenure-track faculty], not just as an issue of equity but rather tied the support to a commitment to students and the goals of the institution around learning. (Kezar, 2013, p. 175)

This is a crucial distinction: efforts to improve contingent faculty working conditions are to benefit not only contingent faculty but also students.

When contingent faculty have job security and a positive environment of professionalism, the quality of education they provide improves. At Northwestern University, mentioned in chapter 2 as an institution that has notably positive labor conditions for contingent faculty, most of the contingent faculty members are long-term employees and have a career ladder with promotional opportunities. In a study of student learning among these contingent faculty members and the tenure-track and tenured faculty, the researchers found that "non-tenure track faculty at Northwestern not only induce students to take more classes in a given subject than do tenure line professors, but also lead the students to do better in subsequent coursework than do their tenure track/tenured colleagues" (Figlio et al., 2015, p. 15). This finding was even stronger for the less prepared students. The authors caution that their findings may not be generalizable to other universities that treat their contingent faculty differently; in other words, they recognize that the contingent faculty at Northwestern are treated better than at most institutions. The concluding words of the study offer hope for campuses where contingent faculty are well treated.

> Certainly learning outcomes are an important consideration in evaluating whether the observed trend away from tenure track/tenured towards non-tenure line faculty is good or bad. Our results provide evidence that the rise of full-time designated teachers at U.S. colleges and universities may be less of a cause for alarm than some people think, and indeed, may actually be educationally beneficial. Perhaps the growing practice of hiring a combination of research-intensive tenure track faculty members and teaching-intensive lecturers may be an efficient and educationally positive solution to a research university's multi-tasking problem. (Figlio et al., 2015, p. 16)

Again, this book takes no position on whether campuses should attempt to convert more contingent lines into tenure lines, or if they should simply elevate contingent career paths into a distinct, yet viable profession. Especially for research universities, increasing the number of full-time permanent positions for teaching-intensive lecturers seems to offer one positive alternative to the exploitation seen at many institutions.

In institutions receiving an A for professional equity, the two-tier system does not weigh as heavily on the minds of those in the lower tier. Although conceptions of upper and lower tracks may still exist, in part because of the nationwide academic culture, the teaching track is largely drained of stigma at A campuses. This creates an environment where contingent faculty can feel the difference, as this contingent lecturer comments in the following: "Administrative and professional support on our department level are very good and I feel that the chairperson and other full-time staff within the

Music Department respect us and are aware of the important role we as adjuncts fill" (House Committee, 2014, p. 24).

An interviewee named Dave, a new contingent faculty member in sociology at a California State University school, contrasted his new role with his previous experience in considerably worse conditions.

> I received an office with my name on the door, a computer, and some administrative support. I received an invitation to the faculty social and to department meetings. They put a bio of me in the department newspaper when I started, and a few of the full-time faculty in the hallways stopped by to introduce themselves and get to know me better. I know I'm not a full professor here, but it is hard not to feel like I belong in a much more profound way than I had felt anywhere before.

Increased professional equity for the contingent faculty workforce has multiple payoffs, the most immediate and direct of which is an increase in the general well-being, satisfaction, and productivity of contingent faculty members themselves. But perhaps the most compelling argument to be made is that increased professionalization of the contingent faculty workforce results in greater engagement in the quality of education delivered in the classroom, as illustrated at Northwestern University (Figlio et al., 2015).

6

Social Equity

Faculty Diversity and Inclusivity by Race and Gender

An institution treating contingent faculty with fair pay and opportunities to advance is still not achieving true equity if it is contributing to continued inequality and segregation across race and gender lines. Academia is already a stressful and competitive field of employment, and it becomes toxic when faculty also shoulder experiences of disparagement or a sense of being tokenized for their race or gender.

Educational leader Barbara Townsend (2009) writes that a positive organizational climate for women and minorities working at colleges has three easy-to-measure indexes: representation of minorities and women faculty members is proportionate to their percentage in the population served by the institution, equal pay for equal work, and equal opportunity for promotion. As society becomes increasingly diverse, greater diversity among our thought leaders must keep pace. Just as student enrollments should be proportionate to the populations being served, proportionate numbers of diverse faculty are also necessary.

A diverse faculty has many women and people of color among contingent ranks as well as tenured and permanent lines. To accurately determine a campus's inclusivity, it is crucial to examine the levels of diversity between contingent and noncontingent faculty. This chapter takes a brief look at some issues and trends on the topic of faculty diversity.

Benefits of a Diverse Faculty

A diverse faculty not only helps avoid group think by drawing in people from divergent backgrounds but also helps students of color feel more included, particularly at predominantly White institutions. Research has shown that minority faculty members contribute to higher minority student retention rates at predominantly White campuses (Jones, Castellanos, & Cole, 2002; Alexander & Moore, 2008). Further, White and minority students self-report that they perceive a more diverse faculty as beneficial to their education on multiple dimensions (Hall & Rivera-Torres, 2011). Alexia, an African American student at a California State University in Northern California, remarked in an interview,

> In my department there are a handful of minority faculty, but no Black faculty. But there are a lot of women. It's funny because I never feel like being a woman is an issue, but sometimes I feel singled out as the only Black person in a class. But my friend is the opposite: she is Asian in a department with lots of Asian faculty, but few women, and she feels self-conscious in reverse. So, I think the issues arise when a student feels like [he or she is] "the only one" along whatever aspect of identity is in question.

Although it is impossible to perfectly balance the faculty of every department at every college along lines of race and gender, especially at smaller departments, taking modest steps toward a faculty that is almost representative of the population it serves is a crucial starting point. As discussed in chapters 7 and 8, the Contingent Labor Conditions Score measures gender and racial equality in faculty membership, as well as material and professional equity.

Categories: Sex, Gender, Race, and Ethnicity

For the Contingent Labor Conditions Score, the racial categories are the same as those used by the U.S. Census and by the U.S. Department of Education (2007). Adopting these categories for the Contingent Labor Conditions Score will allow users of the tool to more easily calculate their benchmarks by accessing publicly available data on population demographics. The respondent is first asked to indicate if he or she is Hispanic or Latino in ethnicity. Then the respondent is prompted to choose his or her racial category from among the following: American Indian or Alaskan Native, Asian, Black or African American, Native Hawaiian or Other Pacific Islander, and White.

Benchmarks

In theory, ideal levels of faculty diversity are fairly straightforward and should match the diversity of the population served. All students, contingent faculty, and tenure-line faculty would be evenly split between men and women. Each of these groups would also be divided racially into proportions matching the demographics of the region and the populations of students served. When taken as a whole, our postsecondary institutions would have proportions of racial diversity that match the proportions of race in the country as a whole. Of course, in practice, determining exactly which ratios best represent the population served is more complicated. For example, should proportionality match nationwide ratios, state ratios, county or city ratios, or something else?

The Contingent Labor Conditions Score suggests that gender ratios should be close to 50:50 (male-female) among contingent faculty and non-contingent faculty. In terms of racial equity, rates of diversity should also be the same between contingent and noncontingent ranks. Further, desirable race ratios are calculated based on three sources: rates of diversity among the student population, in the county, and in the state. This is examined more in the discussion of calculating racial equity in chapter 8 (pp. 91–95). Although this is not the first project to attempt to create a diversity meas-ure, it is unique in that it focuses on a blend of context-specific sources: the student population, the county, and the state. Many other diversity scales or indexes, such as the one from *USA Today* (Meyer & McIntosh, 1999), compare institutions to national averages instead of taking local realities into account.

The Statistics: Sex and Gender

Gender scholars agree that the net progress of feminist goals nationwide has slowed since the 1990s (Cotter, Hermsen, & Vanneman, 2011; England, 2010). Change has come in fits and starts, with progress consolidated in some sectors while leaving other areas virtually untouched. Even in individual institu-tions and occupations, internal inequities exist (Reskin & Padavic, 2002). This is no less true in the academy, where gender parity has been reached in certain areas, but not in others, such as between contingent and noncontingent faculty.

According to the NCES (2016), in 2014 women earned 61% of the 1,006,961 associate degrees awarded and 57% of the 1,840,164 bachelor's degrees awarded. Numbers of female students have consistently surpassed the number of male students in institutions of higher education since the early 1980s. Although gender parity among students has made significant progress, gender parity among faculty has moved more slowly.

Female faculty made up only 36% of total faculty in 1991 but increased to 49% by 2013 (NCES, 2016). Nevertheless, gender bias in academic hiring is a documented reality (Corrice, 2009), and as shown in Table 6.1, gender equity varies markedly across role and institutional type. Although

TABLE 6.1

**Percentages of U.S. Faculty Who Are Female Across Ranks and Types,
2013 and 2003**

Full-Time Only, All Institutional Types (2013) (%)	All Institutional Types (2003) (%)	Public Research Universities (2003) (%)	Public Two-Year Colleges (2003) (%)
Full Professor Rank	Full-Time, All Ranks	Full-Time, All Ranks	Full-Time, All Ranks
30.7	38.3	30.1	49.5
Instructor Rank	Part-Time, All Ranks	Part-Time, All Ranks	Part-Time, All Ranks
56.8	47.9	49.6	49.3

Note. From NCES (2016). For 2013 data, see Table 315.20. For 2003 data, see Table 315.50.

the data in Table 6.1 were published in 2016, the table reveals faculty data much older, particularly the 2003 data, because the U.S. Department of Education program tracking these statistics (i.e., stats about gender, race, and status of part-time faculty) was defunded after the 2003 data was released. In 2003 women had achieved gender parity among two-year college faculty but trailed in higher tier institutions to only 30% of faculty in public research universities. Although the 2013 data do not show us statistics on part-time faculty, the fact that women made up only 30.7% of all faculty holding full professor rank tells us that not much progress was made over that decade.

The Statistics: Race and Ethnicity

Issues of racial privilege and prejudice in the professoriate are ongoing, demonstrated by extensive literature (Milem, Chang, & Antonio, 2005; Smith, Altbach, & Lomotey, 2002). Table 6.2 covers some basic figures for racial groups in higher education. Notice that some groups have faculty representation above their ratio of the overall population, like Whites (63.7% to 72.7%) and Asians (4.9% to 9.1%), while other populations have significantly lower faculty representation than their percentage of the overall population, like Hispanics (16.3% to 4.2%) and Blacks (12.2% to 5.5%). Also, note that this type of data on part-time faculty has not been tracked by the NCES since 2003.

Also revealing is a comparison between the proportions of part-time to full-time faculty within each racial or ethnic grouping. According to the

TABLE 6.2

Racial Group Representation in Higher Education (All Institutional Types)

Race	U.S. Population, 2010 Census (n = 308,745,538)[a] (%)	Students, Graduate and Undergraduate 2014 (n = 20,207,400)[b] (%)	All Faculty, 2013 (n = 791,391)[c] (%)	Part-Time Faculty 2003 (n = 530,000)[d] (%)
White	63.7	55.6	72.7	85.2
Hispanic or Latino	16.3	15.8	4.2	3.5
Black or African American	12.2	13.8	5.5	5.6
Asian and Pacific Islander	4.9	6.3	9.1	3.9
American Indian or Alaska Native	0.7	0.8	0.5	1.8
Two or more races	1.9	3.2	0.7	n/a
Race or ethnicity unknown	n/a	n/a	2.5	n/a

Note. [a]From U.S. Census Bureau (n.d.). [b]From National Center for Education Statistics (2016); see Table 306.10, which also lists another 4.5% of nonresident alien students. [c]From National Center for Education Statistics (2016); see Table 315.20, which also lists 4.9% of nonresident alien faculty. [d]From National Center for Education Statistics (2016), see Table 315.60; these percentages do not include two or more, unknown, or alien categories.

NCES (2016), in 2003, 43.7% of all faculty were part-time (530,000 out of 1,211,800). From a racial equality standpoint, we should ideally see similar ratios across racial categories. Unfortunately, the distribution can be very uneven (see Table 6.3). For example, only 24.6% of Asian faculty held part-time positions, whereas 49.2% of American Indian faculty did.

Change will not happen by accident. Smith, Turner, Osei-Kofi, and Richards (2004) show that intentional practices are necessary for hiring a diverse faculty. Jayakumar, Howard, Allen, and Han (2009) reveal that underrepresentation is not only a recruitment issue but also a retention and satisfaction issue. Weinberg (2008) argues that non-White faculty should not be primarily consolidated into single departments (e.g., ethnic studies), because if departments do not have internal diversity, pockets of segregation grow on campuses.

TABLE 6.3
Percentage of Part-Time Faculty by Racial Group, 2003

Race	Part-Time (%)
All Faculty	43.7
White	45.2
Hispanic or Latino	44.0
Black or African American	43.8
Asian and Pacific Islander	24.6
American Indian or Alaska Native	49.2

Note. From National Center for Education Statistics (2016), see Table 315.50.

Gender Equity Perspectives

Because of the overall progress in academia over the past several decades, gender imbalances among faculty have diminished considerably. Nevertheless, they still exist in pockets across the country, especially in male-dominated fields and in the number of women who are adjuncts compared to full professors. One female faculty member at University of California, Los Angeles's Anderson School of Management, where women were only 14.3% of tenured faculty in 2013, reported on the issue in *Newsweek*:

> It's a little like radiation poisoning—there are all these little instances, and over time they build up and kill you. . . . We were hearing stories about times when [female faculty] were disregarded or told they weren't good enough. Over time, these little things that everyone ignores add up. (Suddath, 2014, para. 9)

Of course, just the presence of female faculty does not solve all the issues, especially if women are not represented equally in the higher- and lower-ranking positions.

> You will probably find a majority of adjuncts to be bright, highly educated women. . . . Students are receiving an excellent education from instructors who are highly educated, committed to education, experienced and world wise, but who are not models or examples of success in higher education, especially older women. Female students suffer when some of the best women teachers are an underclass in higher ed. (House Committee, 2014, p. 29)

Answers are not easy to come by, as one female faculty member learned when she attended a conference workshop on advancing female careers in academia. After noticing that all the advice seemed to be directed only to tenure-track faculty, she asked,

> How does the multiple marginalization of women contingent scholars lead to a lack of opportunity for advancement, and what can be done about it? What institutional reforms and policies would the panelists recommend to allow contingent faculty greater mobility? (Harrison-Kahan, 2014, para. 15)

To her dismay, the panelists were stumped. As University of California, Berkeley psychologist Alison Gopnick asserts,

> If ever there was a women's issue in the academy, this is it. Adjuncting is where the so-called Mommy Track is. A lot of women think they can have families and stay in the game by adjuncting. They get trapped there. (Hacker & Dreifus, 2011, p. 54)

Gender inequality is likely to be more insidious in certain disciplines, such as those that attract more male applicants (e.g., theology, engineering, computer science, and economics). In these cases, people on hiring committees need to think hard about how they contribute to the reification of inequality if they do not seek greater equity. Having more female faculty members has been shown to attract more female students to a department, especially in underrepresented science, technology, engineering, and mathematics fields (Sonnert, Fox, & Adkins, 2007).

Racial Equity Perspectives

The need for greater racial diversity in many U.S. college faculties is painfully obvious at certain institutions that are completely out of balance with the ratios of students they have or the makeup of their communities. After a survey at Brandeis University found that Black and Hispanic professors made up an abysmal 3.4% of tenure-track faculty, one Black professor lamented to the *Boston Globe* about repeatedly losing quality students to schools with a more diverse faculty: "Often, students want to know that there will be someone like them they can talk to within a department, that they're not just going to a white school" (Jan, 2010, para. 17).

One dean at the same university tried to send a message to hiring committees by posting photos of the entire faculty along walls of a central hall on campus, saying, "I wanted them to look in the mirror and see that this was not a diverse faculty" (Jan, 2010, para. 11).

Julie Withers, a multiracial adjunct from Butte Community College in California, was infuriated when an executive member of the academic senate dismissed the campus's lack of faculty diversity with the statement, "They don't like living in rural areas" (Withers, 2016, para. 5). She wrote the following in an open forum:

> Who is "they?" If you are one of "them," then you know that they are talking about people of color. . . . Again, the composition of our faculty is not reflective of our service area, nor does it uphold the organization's mission of equal employment opportunities. People who get the job at this campus look like the people hiring them; they must "fit." . . . It is a white assumption that people of color do not like living in rural areas. Rural areas themselves, trees and dirt, are not especially threatening. It is the hostility and rejection, knowing that one . . . must leave their true self at the door. (Withers, 2016, para. 5)

To be fair, in most cases hiring committees do not intentionally try to create racial inequality, but until they intentionally take steps to solve it, they are still deserving of criticism.

Some of the most respected and resourced universities in the country cite disturbingly low Latino faculty numbers, such as the University of Pennsylvania with 1.8%, Cornell with 3.2%, and Stanford with 4% (Zhu, 2014). After the failed efforts of a 10-year diversity initiative at Duke University, academic council chair Joshua Socolar said, "The total number [of Latino faculty] right now is not great" (Zhu, 2014, para. 3) at 2%, or 35 out of the 1,768 tenured faculty. "We don't want to say we're doing fine if all our Latino faculty are doing Latino studies" (Zhu, 2014, para. 14) as this creates a kind of relegation within the university. Using the Contingent Labor Conditions Score, the benchmark for Duke University Latino faculty should be around 9%, based on a Latino student population of 6%, Durham County with 13.5%, and North Carolina at 8.4%.

One Latino contingent faculty member at Duke University said, "If we don't include concrete criteria [for selecting] people who are different from us, people are going to keep choosing themselves" (Zhu, 2014, para. 20). Inderdeep Chatrath, director of affirmative action and equal opportunity at the Office of Institutional Equity at Duke University, adds that finding Latino faculty is a particular challenge in the university's region but mentions new initiatives, including adding 13 Latino postdocs in hopes of mentoring some into tenure-track positions. "It is not something that we can take care of in one year or even five years, but I am encouraged by the fact that we are doing something," Chatrath said (Zhu, 2014, para. 23). These efforts are supported by findings that having a critical mass of Latino faculty has positive academic outcomes for Latino students (Hagedorn, Chi, Cepeda, & McLain, 2007).

Striving for an A in Gender and Racial Equity

Campuses that have achieved balance along gender and racial lines deserve to celebrate, as this sets an example for other schools. These institutions should be quick to promote their best practices in workshops, at professional associations, and in white papers or journal articles.

When gender and racial equity characterize the faculty ranks among contingent and permanent positions, the impacts will be felt at all levels of the university. More hiring committees will have diverse faculty, and the odds of diverse administrators rising from those ranks will also increase.

Unfortunately, finding reports of positive experiences are few and far between. In a report on the experiences of faculty of color at Western Washington University, there were mixed responses, although one person did say the following about the progress in the department culture:

> I can honestly say I believe that we have a . . . department where the issue of diversity and social justice, every faculty member that we have in our program, understands. . . . I couldn't have always said that. To me, that is really important as a person in one of those underappreciated groups. (Dozier, 2014, p. 6)

Similarly, in another study about the experiences of female faculty in academic medicine in which most of the responses were not as positive as the previous comment, examples of empowerment do exist, as in the following:

> The most positive, really acute turning point in the advancement of my career was an annual performance review with my Chair many years ago. And she asked me, "What do you want to do in 5 years? Do you want to be a department chair, a dean, what is it you want to do?" And she not only asked me the question but she actually meant it, to the point where she made suggestions over time and gave me responsibilities, and asked me if I would do certain things that forced me to build my experience and credentials in a variety of leadership roles. (Pololi & Jones, 2010, p. 443)

Of course, despite the successes of A institutions, remember that the benchmarks are based on contextual factors, which will be different across the country. Campuses in areas that have little racial diversity may achieve an

A grade with a relatively homogenous demographic makeup. For example, many institutions may achieve a benchmark for Native Americans and Alaska Natives of 1%. Nationwide, that would be about an average number. But suppose a campus has a faculty of about 1,000; in that case 1% only represents 10 faculty members. Further, those 10 people may be from a variety of different tribal groups. A campus may earn an A for racial equity on the Contingent Labor Conditions Score because of the strides it has taken to support diversity, but this does not mean that some faculty will not experience being very much in the minority on campus. The Contingent Labor Conditions Score measures basic campus composition and instructor ratios, but it does not measure the climate of respect, support, and collegiality experienced by minority populations. Nevertheless, it is a starting point for these conversations.

The Contingent Labor Conditions Score creates a regionally contextual benchmark. For a more complex look at minority experience, once the whole Contingent Labor Conditions Score has been calculated, it will be easy to go back and look at the professional identity score for particular racial or gender categories. Examining these data for specific demographic categories will provide additional insights into the sense of job satisfaction and collegiality experienced by various subgroups on campus.

Part Three

The Contingent Labor Conditions Score

The following two chapters focus on an instrument for institutional self-assessment, the Contingent Labor Conditions Score. It is described in chapter 7, which briefly summarizes its three primary sections: material, professional, and social equity. In chapter 8, formulas, tables, and survey items necessary to calculate an institution's score are explained with examples. This final section of the book proposes a standardized tool for grading labor practices toward contingent faculty at individual colleges and universities. It is most useful at institutions where doctoral teaching assistants are not assigned the largest portion of contingent instruction.

7

Introducing the Contingent Labor Conditions Score

The Contingent Labor Conditions Score is a rating tool to gauge the conditions that contingent faculty experience at their institution of higher education. The score can be calculated in three main areas, each of which contains subareas. The scores on the three main areas can be averaged for an overall grade of the institution's contingent labor conditions. The following are the three main components of the Contingent Labor Conditions Score:

1. Material equity: Pay parity, job security, and benefits
2. Professional equity: Professional opportunity and professional identity
3. Social equity: inclusiveness of gender and race

The material and social equity grades are calculated without using a survey instrument, whereas half of the professional equity grade is based on surveying contingent faculty members. This chapter offers an overview of the tool and discusses the methodology used to design it. Once calculated, grading for each of the three areas (as well as the overall score) follows a traditional academic scale, shown in Table 7.1.

Although many ways of representing the outcomes could be employed, an education-style grading scale is apropos and intuitively understood by nearly all who have gone through formal education. As is typical with any report card, F is failure, and D is on the threshold of failure. Although C is technically average, it is rarely considered a good mark. B is above average but with

TABLE 7.1
Grading Scale

Grade	Range	Grade	Range	Grade	Range	Grade	Range	Grade	Range
A	93–100	B+	87–89	C+	77–79	D+	67–69	F	00–59
A–	90–92	B	83–86	C	73–76	D	63–66		
		B–	80–82	C–	70–72	D–	60–62		

clear room for improvement. Of course an A indicates excellence. Table 7.2 shows a completed Contingent Labor Conditions Score with grades.

Material Equity: Pay Parity, Job Security, and Employee Benefits

While pay is perhaps the most obvious form of material equity, the Contingent Labor Conditions Score also takes into account job security and benefits.

Pay Parity

This portion of the instrument focuses on pay parity for contingent faculty members compared to tenure-track faculty members. One of the primary reasons colleges hire contingent faculty is that they cost the institution significantly less. As campuses grow dependent on cheap labor to manage costs, they risk becoming more fiscally bound to the practice. Furthermore, low wages can lead to a low quality of life personally and professionally for contingent faculty that can, in turn, have a negative impact on students.

Job Security

Beyond pay equity, another way to improve basic material conditions for contingent faculty is to offer some measure of job security. Although tenure has long been held as the faculty gold standard for security of employment in academia, it is not the only alternative to a term-by-term contract. Institutions with more robust formulations of rehire rights, such as systems of vestment, seniority, priority of assignment, and so on, score higher. Greater job security incentivizes employees to make longer-term investments in the institution. The leading example to date is the system at VCC, where part-time faculty have job security based on seniority, calculated equally to that of full-time faculty.

Employee Benefits

Finally, employees are greatly served by some portion of the benefits allotted to full-time faculty. These typically includes health and retirement benefits, and sometimes other kinds of benefits (e.g., sick days, vacation leave).

Professional Equity: Opportunity and Identity

This part of the Contingent Labor Conditions Score is used to calculate two related areas. The professional opportunity section is based on the objective policies of the institution toward contingent faculty. The professional identity section, in contrast, is based on the subjective experiences of contingent faculty members working at the institution.

TABLE 7.2

Visual Hierarchy of Contingent Labor Conditions Scores: Example

Contingent Labor Conditions Score: 81%, B–						
Material Equity Grade: 78%, C+			Professional Equity Grade: 81%, B–		Social Equity Grade: 83%, B	
Pay Parity Grade: 83%, B	Job Security Grade: 78%, C+	Benefits Grade: 74%, C	Professional Opportunity Grade: 85%, B	Professional Identity Grade: 77%, C+	Gender Equity Grade: 95%, A	Racial Equity Grade: 71%, C–
• Pay per course comparable to noncontingent faculty	• Rehire rights • Consistency of assignment • Allowance for breaks in service • Grievance process	• Medical • Retirement • Dental • Vision • Allowances for dependents	• Professional development • Opportunities for advancement • Academic freedom	• Sense of inclusion and job satisfaction	• Gender representation in proportion to population served	• Racial representation in proportion to population served

Note. The scores or grade percentages in this table are for illustrative purposes only.

Professional Opportunity

The Contingent Labor Conditions Score takes into account opportunities for growth, from on-campus training or mentorship programs to funds for association memberships and conference participation. Furthermore, when a full-time position does become available, is priority consideration given to current contingent faculty, or is seniority a consideration? In short, are there reasonable opportunities for advancement and promotion? Full tenure-track jobs are not the only option for promotion; well-compensated lecturer roles with job security are an enormous improvement over the general status of most contingent faculty members. In any case, layoff and grievance rights are a significant component of professionalization, as opposed to a powerless and transient faculty.

Professional Identity

In this section, the Contingent Labor Conditions Score focuses on the perspectives of the contingent faculty members themselves. To what degree do contingent faculty feel they are offered departmental inclusion? This may include orientation for new hires to the campus and department, introductions to the other faculty, designated office space, a bio on the institution's website, basic administrative support, invitations to department events, and inclusion in shared governance (especially compensated inclusion). Professional identity also extends to issues of collegiality and respect from the noncontingent members of the department. Do contingent faculty have a sense of inclusion in the academic community? Remember that many of the contingent faculty throughout this book reported feeling anonymous. To calculate professional identity, a survey of contingent faculty asking them to evaluate their experiences at the campus in question is required (see the survey in Tables 8.8 and 8.9).

Social Equity: Gender and Race

This section focuses on long-raised questions of diversity and inclusion applied to contingent faculty members.

Gender

Women and people of color made up 58% of temporary instructors, but only 25% of full professors (Weiss & Pankin, 2011). Schell (1998) points out that women are largely overrepresented among contingent faculty who teach introductory composition. General education classes like these are most often assigned to contingent faculty, and too often contingent faculty members are disproportionately female. In other words, it is important to parse the ratios of contingent versus tenure-track faculty by gender and race. Are women included in equal proportions to men among the contingent and noncontingent faculty ranks? Imagine a college with a 50:50 split between male and female faculty. Yet at this same college, what if women represented the majority of the contingent faculty members but only a fraction of the full-time or tenure-track assignments? The average gender ratio of faculty may turn out somewhere near 50:50, but it would be a clearly deceptive equity. The Contingent Labor Conditions Score accounts for this.

Race

Are people of color represented in the faculty ratios, full-time and part time, in similar proportion to the population served by their institution? Population served is a benchmark that differs by campus. The Contingent Labor Conditions Score takes into account the demographics of the student population as well as the regional (county and state) demographics. This creates a more accurate picture of success or failure in hiring for diversity than nationwide benchmarks, which do not take into account regional variation.

A Tapestry of Conditions

These different areas of equity interweave to create the actual conditions experienced by faculty at an institution. For example, low pay parity is exacerbated when there is no opportunity for advancement over time, which is even worse when the unfair situation is concentrated among women or ethnic minorities. The intersection of these labor conditions amplifies their potentially problematic nature.

These threads are important to tease out because it is not part-time or contingent employment itself that is inherently a problem but rather a series of additional conditions in the employment situation that may make it so (Kezar, 2013). Research on the psychological impact of part-time work is mixed, and plenty of examples exist where part-time work is linked to positive psychological outcomes (e.g., Conway & Briner, 2002; Fields & Thacker, 1991). So it is not fair to rate an institution poorly simply for use of part-time faculty. Many different moving parts make the institutional environment more or less equitable, and change can come in various forms (Berry, 2005; Kezar 2012; Kezar & Sam 2013). Thus there is value in the ability to rate an institution on these items together, as well as separately as needed, allowing for more context-specific policy development. Contingent Labor Conditions Scores are calculated with these issues taken into account.

Internal Versus External Assessment

The best situation is when an institution chooses to self-evaluate without external pressure. This may be initiated by the administration, through special task forces or possibly the faculty senate. As is often stated, knowledge is power. Self-evaluation is a very important way of identifying areas for growth or policy reform before contingent morale hits bottom, before student learning is affected, before negative publicity strikes, and before fierce labor negotiations become imminent. Unfortunately, self-audits come most often when external pressure is applied for accountability, such as from accrediting bodies, funding or regulatory agencies, or workers' unions.

The Contingent Labor Conditions Score is prepared under the assumption that the initiator of the instrument has basic access to institutional data and contact with the faculty for the purpose of surveying them (though surveying is only necessary for the second half of the professional equity score). Nevertheless, most of the sections of the Contingent Labor Conditions Score can be completed using data that campuses make publicly available on their websites (especially from their institutional research departments) or from required reporting like the NCES's IPEDS. Of course, if for some reason necessary data cannot be found, survey numbers can be a last-resort substitute, keeping in mind that all survey methodology introduces additional margins of error.

Finally, the Contingent Labor Conditions Score contains multiple sections that can be analyzed in isolation, which means the tool can also be used to calculate only the area or areas of greatest interest to the evaluator. This is useful for those who may not want to conduct surveys because of time, access, or money. (Again, note that only one portion of the professional equity score requires contingent faculty surveying.) This possible piecemeal approach is also beneficial to those who cannot access requisite bits of data; they simply complete what they can.

Notes on Constructing the Instrument

The initial step in constructing the Contingent Labor Conditions Score was a literature review. Many of these sources can be found in the references section of this volume. In addition, existing contingent faculty surveys and instruments were reviewed.

Analyzing Existing Surveys

I conducted an extensive Internet search to find as many publicly posted contingent faculty surveys as possible for comparison of content and approach. Most institutions take time to survey their faculty at some point. Dozens of examples on the Internet include surveys about professional development needs, working conditions, faculty perspectives on student engagement, benefits and compensation satisfaction, feelings about the workplace environment, and more. Some are hosted by organizations with a national scope, such as the Coalition on the Academic Workforce and the Higher Education Research Institute at the University of California, Los Angeles. However, most examples of faculty surveys come from individual colleges. Typically, they are conducted by a task force commissioned by the faculty senate or other campus entity, an outside consultant, the faculty union or as part of routine data collection by internal units, such as institutional research offices. More rare are surveys specifically focused on contingent or part-time faculty.

After extensive searching, I found 32 surveys specific to contingent faculty. Three were conducted by community college districts, 3 by national organizations, 2 as part of doctoral dissertations, 1 by a government agency, 1 by a faculty union, 1 by an individual department, and the rest (21) by a campuswide entity (e.g., institutional research office, office of the provost, professional development office). Five of the surveys had specifically narrow topics of focus, but the remaining 27 contained questions across a broad range of topics. The most common categories or themes of questioning tended to be centered in one of the following 6 areas:

1. Demographics: Race, gender, age, years of experience, and level of education
2. Satisfaction: With students, work conditions, available support services, and more
3. Resources: What support individual departments were providing, such as computers, phones, office space, orientations, and invitations to meetings
4. Professional development: Training considered most helpful and future support that would be helpful
5. Students and teaching and learning: Questions about faculty impressions of student readiness, engagement, learning, and pedagogical

methods (e.g., do the faculty use discussion groups, presentations, lectures, clickers, online or hybrid courses, or written assignments?)

6. Campus climate: Less common than the preceding items, a few surveys included questions about how the campus was experienced by faculty in terms of issues like safety, racism, sexism, and collegiality

Although no individual questions were copied and pasted into the Contingent Labor Conditions Score, the ability to see what administrators of institutions are asking across the United States proved illuminating. The reviewed surveys informed the inclusion of key items in the Contingent Labor Conditions Score. Therefore, the tool covers the primary areas of nationwide concern. Some who use the Contingent Labor Conditions Score may wish additional items were included, so users of the tool are invited to view it as a threshold or base set of information that can be built on for their own institution.

Although many other parts could have been added, the Contingent Labor Conditions Score was designed to be as short as possible and rely on minimal surveying in an effort to create a tool with little associated expense to the organizations or individuals using it. That being said, some campus leaders may wish to add a few additional items to the survey portion to capture useful information in the previously mentioned areas. If recommendations are needed for specific questions, readers are encouraged to review the Contingent Academic Workforce (2012) survey, the Higher Education Research Institute (2017) faculty survey, and the 2013 Public Sociology/Contingent Faculty Working Conditions Survey (Public Sociology Department, George Mason University, 2013).

Constructing Categories

Finally, a few words are in order on the business of constructing categories on gender, race, and ethnicity. Inclusive and open-ended categories are valued because of the fluid nature of social constructions such as gender and race. Nevertheless, the challenge in quantitative instrument design is to create categories broad enough for statistical comparisons, even if the result is a less than ideal reflection of reality. For this reason, the gender and race categories used in this instrument are based on the categories used by the U.S. Census Bureau (n.d.b.) and the U.S. Department of Education (2007).

The next chapter is a step-by-step discussion on how to calculate the Contingent Labor Conditions Score.

8

Calculating the Contingent Labor Conditions Score

This chapter demonstrates how to calculate step-by-step the material, professional, and social equity grades of the Contingent Labor Conditions Score, which is designed as an assessment tool for campus leaders who wish to track and improve labor practices for non-tenure-track faculty. Blank versions of the tables used to calculate the various example components of the Contingent Labor Conditions Score can be found in the Appendix or online. The online version includes an Excel workbook that does all of the calculations for you. These resources are available at https://sty.presswarehouse.com/books/BookDetail.aspx?productID=412424.

Calculating Pay Parity, Job Security, Benefits, and the Overall Material Equity Grade

This section contains examples and explanations of how to calculate the overall material equity grade. Pay parity, job security, and benefits are first calculated separately, then averaged to arrive at the total material equity score.

Calculating Pay Parity

The logic of the formula is discussed here, but in short the equation for calculating pay parity is the following:

(Average contingent faculty pay per course × 10) ÷ (Average lowest tier tenure-track-faculty pay per year × .75)

Step 1

We begin with the denominator because we need a modest base number to compare contingent faculty pay with tenure-track pay. Determine the average rate of pay for incoming tenure-track faculty members at the lowest step or rank at your institution, which is usually new assistant professors.[1]

If the lowest pay rate is different across disciplines, use the average of the numbers. Also, some campuses may have outliers, such as unusually high pay used to attract celebrity or superstar faculty; ignore those additional exceptions for these purposes, as they skew the data.

Now multiply the average rate of tenure-track pay by 75%. Tenure-track faculty members have additional administrative and service responsibilities that are not expected of contingent faculty. In addition to a full teaching load, they work about 25% more because of administrative expectations. Again, this ratio is debatable, but it provides a fairly standard estimate for cross-institutional comparison (see chapter 4 for more rationale on the 75% ratio).

Step 2

To derive the numerator, start by identifying the average pay per course for contingent faculty at the institution in question. Then multiply the average contingent faculty pay per course by 10, which imitates a 5-5 full-time teaching load, or 5 courses in the fall semester and 5 courses in the semester.

A 5-5 load may seem high, but it is very common at teaching-intensive institutions. A 5-5 load equals 30 semester units at most campuses. Note that most institutions calculate 1 semester unit with 1.5 quarter units, so 30 semester units are 45 quarter units. Even if the institution has a unit cap for part-time faculty, it is still necessary to multiply by 10 to get a figure equivalent to that of tenure-track faculty.

Step 3

Now divide the numerator by the denominator. Round to two decimal points, and then convert the resulting decimal to a percentage. This is the pay parity of the institution, and one of three scores that will go into calculating the total material equity grade.

For example, let's say the salary for the lowest step for tenure-track faculty at the institution in question is $65,000. Apply the 75% parity definition, reducing $65,000 to $48,750. Further, suppose the college pays contingent faculty $3,500 per course. Multiply $3,500 by 10 (for a 5-5 load). The resulting figure is $35,000. Then, divide $35,000 by $48,750, resulting in .72 (rounded to two decimal points), or a pay parity score of 72%, which would be a grade of C–. The following is an example of this calculation:

(Average contingent faculty pay per course × 10) ÷ (Average lowest tier tenure-track-faculty pay per year × .75)

$3,500 × 10 = $35,000

$65,000 × .75 = $48, 750

$35,000 ÷ $48,750 = .72 (rounded) or 72% (C–)

It is recommended you use this score to measure how your institution is performing on this particular metric (pay parity) as well as how it is doing overall with material equity. The pay parity score is averaged with job security and benefits performance, as explained in the following section.

Calculating Job Security

Use Table 8.1 (following page) to calculate the job security metric. You will have to be familiar with the college's rehire rights, cancellation compensation, and so on to properly score its performance in this category.

The most important item is rehire rights, which is worth four times more than the four items following it (consistency of assignment, breaks in service, cancellation compensation, and grievance process). The total score can range from 0 to 24. Later, this score will be divided by 24 to yield a decimal used to calculate the material equity grade (more on that later).

Total points earned ÷ 24

As with pay parity, it is recommended that you gauge the institution's performance on this particular issue of job security as well as eventually using it to find the overall material equity score.

TABLE 8.1

Job Security Items: Example

Item	None 0 Points	Weak 4 Points	Moderate 8 Points	Strong 12 Points	
Rehire rights	None	Preferential hiring of returning instructors after 3 years (6 semesters, 9 quarters) of service	Preferential hiring of returning instructors immediately or before 3 years	Preferential hiring of returning instructors within 3 years, plus allowance for multiyear renewable contracts	Points: 12

Item	None 0 Points	Weak 1 Point	Moderate 2 Points	Strong 3 Points	
Consistency of assignment	By convenience of chair or scheduler	Explicitly stated policy allowances for consistency of courses or scheduling, but not both	Explicitly stated policy allowances for consistency of courses and scheduling	Additional point if tenure-track faculty cannot override returning part-time faculty for overtime load	Points: 0
Breaks in service	Not allowed	Only for documented hardships, faculty must get approval for allowance, rehire rights may be partially diminished	Rare breaks in service allowed without hardship documentation, rehire rights may be partially diminished	Seniority-based system allowing occasional breaks in service without diminishing seniority	Points: 3
Cancellation compensation	Not compensated	Compensated less than 50%	Compensated at 50% or higher	Additional point if a 30-plus day notification of termination is required	Points: 1
Grievance process	No explicitly written process	Written, but no representative designated to support it	Written, and human resources representative or administrator is the support contact	Written, and an elected faculty or union representative is the support contact	Points: 2
				Total points earned: ___18	

Note. Data in this table are fictitious for visual illustration.

Calculating Benefits

Use Table 8.2 (following page) to calculate the benefits metric. The most important benefits are medical and retirement, which is why they are scored much higher (ranging from 0 to 9 points) than the other items: dental, vision, and access to dependents (ranging from 0 to 2 points each). The total score can range from 0 to 24.

Again, reflect on the institution's score on this specific metric. In a moment, you'll divide it by 24 to get a decimal that will be used to calculate the overall material equity performance.

TABLE 8.2
Benefits Items: Example

Benefit	None	Low	Modest	High	
Points :	0	3	6	9	
Medical	Not offered, or available, but employee is responsible for full cost	Available, with 0%–33% of costs covered by employer	Available, with 34%–66% of costs covered by employer	Available, with 67%–100% of costs covered by employer	Points: 9
Retirement	Not offered, or available, but no contribution matching	Available, with contribution matching up to 2%	Available, with contribution matching of 3%–4%	Available, with contribution matching of 5% or more	Points: 6
Points:	0		1	2	
Dental	Not offered, or available, but employee is responsible for the full cost		Available, costs are split between the employer and employee	Available, employer covers full cost	Points: 2
Vision	Not offered, or available, but employee is responsible for the full cost		Available, costs are split between the employer and employee	Available, employer covers full cost	Points: 2
Dependents on medical benefits	Not offered, or allows dependents, but at full cost to employee		Allows dependents, partially subsidized	Allows dependents, subsidized at same rate as employee	Points: 1
				Total points earned: 20	

Note. Data in this table are fictitious for visual illustration.

Calculating Total Material Equity Grade

Take the results from the three previous formulas.

Pay parity: (Average contingent faculty pay per course × 10) ÷ (Average lowest tier tenure-track-faculty pay per year × .75)

Job security: total points earned ÷ 24

Benefits: total points earned ÷ 24

Each produces a decimal between 0 and 1. Round each calculation to two decimal points (e.g., 0.81). Find the average of these three decimals. Next, convert the resulting decimal to a percentage and place it in the grading scale in Table 8.3. The result is the institution's grade for material equity.

For example, if the institution earned a pay-parity ratio of .72 as in the previous example, plus 18 job security points and 20 benefits points, as shown in Tables 8.1 and 8.2, this would be calculated as follows:

Pay parity ratio: .72

Job security points: 18 ÷ 24 = .75

Benefits points: 20 ÷ 24 = .83

All three averaged together yields the following:

.72 + .75 + .83 = 2.30

2.30 ÷ 3 = .77

With a total material equity grade of .77, or 77%, the institution would earn a letter grade of C+ according to Table 8.3. (When calculating the overall percentage for the three main components of the Contingent Labor Conditions Score, round any score ending in .5 or higher up to the next whole number or round down if it is below .5; e.g., 92.3% would be rounded down to 92%.)

TABLE 8.3
Grading Scale

Grade	Range	Grade	Range	Grade	Range	Grade	Range	Grade	Range
A	93–100	B+	87–89	C+	77–79	D+	67–69	F	00–59
A–	90–92	B	83–86	C	73–76	D	63–66		
		B–	80–82	C–	70–72	D–	60–62		

Calculating Professional Opportunity, Professional Identity, and the Overall Professional Equity Grade

This section contains instructions and examples for calculating the three sub-parts of professional opportunity, how to survey contingent faculty to arrive at the professional identity score, and how to calculate the overall professional equity grade. Note that although the professional opportunity score can be calculated with institutional-level data, calculating the professional identity score requires surveying faculty.

Calculating Professional Opportunity

Professional opportunity has three parts: professional development, opportunity for advancement, and academic freedom. Each part is scored according to the example point tallies and calculations provided in Tables 8.4, 8.5, and 8.6. It is recommended that you determine your institution's performance in each category. Later, each of those separate category scores will be used to calculate the overall professional opportunity score as well as the professional equity grade.

If access to the information required for calculating a professional opportunity score (as shown in Tables 8.4, 8.5, and 8.6) is not available, then include those items in the survey sent to contingent faculty. The faculty members can then provide the missing data.

The score for professional development (Table 8.4) is the sum total of points from the four types of opportunities for professional development, divided by four. The resulting decimal can be converted to a percentage to get its individual grade standing but is also used later in the total calculation of the professional equity grade.

The score for opportunity for advancement (Table 8.5) is the sum total of points from the four support mechanisms for advancement, divided by four. Again, the resulting decimal can be converted to a percentage to get its individual grade standing but is also used later in the total calculation of the professional equity grade.

The academic freedom score (Table 8.6) is the sum total of points from the three forms of academic freedom, divided by three. The resulting decimal can be converted to a percentage to get its individual grade standing but, like the previous two, is used later in the total calculation of the professional equity grade.

Keep this and the other two professional opportunity scores handy, as they will all be needed to calculate the total professional opportunity score and the overall professional equity grade.

TABLE 8.4
Professional Development: Example

Opportunities for Contingent Faculty	0 Points	5 Points	10 Points	
New employee orientation	Not available	Offered by some departments	Offered to all as a centralized resource	Points: 10
On-campus workshops and training	Not available (or only about policy compliance)	Offered by some departments	Offered to all as a centralized resource	Points: 5
Funds for conference travel or professional memberships	Not available	Offered by some departments	Offered to all as a centralized resource	Points: 10
Shared governance roles	Not available	Departmental level (or lower level university task forces and committees)	University level (academic senate or other top curriculum and employment policy committees)	Points: 5
			Total points earned: ___30___ ÷ 4 = Total Score: ___7.5___	

Note. Data in this table are fictitious for visual illustration.

TABLE 8.5
Opportunity for Advancement: Example

Support Mechanisms for Advancement	0 points	5 points	10 points	
Statistics of past conversions from contingent to permanent roles are kept updated and available*	Not available	In some cases	Consistently	Points: 10
Information is available that explains what the selection criteria will be when permanent roles open up	Not available	In some cases	Consistently	Points: 10

(*Continued*)

TABLE 8.5 (*Continued*)

Support Mechanisms for Advancement	0 points	5 points	10 points	
When new full-time positions open up, current qualified contingent faculty are given priority for an interview	Not available	In some cases	Consistently	Points: 10
There is consideration of seniority in the selection process when a permanent position becomes available	Not available	In some cases	Consistently	Points: 5
			Total points: ___35___ ÷ 4 = Total score: __8.75__	

Note. Available statistics of past conversions from contingent to permanent roles is about transparency. Having that data available helps contingent faculty make better choices about how long to stay at a campus given the relative odds of eventually becoming permanent. Data in this table are fictitious for visual illustration.

TABLE 8.6
Academic Freedom: Example

Available Forms of Academic Freedom for Contingent Faculty	0 points	5 points	10 points	
Write their own syllabi with choice of texts, assignments, and assessments	Not available	In some cases	Consistently	Points: 10
A statement on academic freedom exists in an official document (e.g., employee handbook, union contract, or campus policy)	Not available	Vaguely written	Clearly written	Points: 10
Mechanisms exist to respond to student complaints about faculty for academic reasons (e.g., lecture content or grades given)	Not available	Vaguely written	Clearly written	Points: 5
			Total points: ___25___ ÷ 3 = Total score: __8.33__	

Note. Data in this table are fictitious for visual illustration.

Calculating Professional Opportunity

Before calculating the overall professional equity grade, find the percentage for professional opportunity. The three sections that constitute professional opportunity (i.e., professional development, opportunity for advancement, and academic freedom) are averaged as shown with the example numbers from previous tables compiled in Table 8.7.

Calculating the scores for the professional opportunity and professional identity sections separately allows comparing the objective or structural features of the campus (the professional opportunity items) with the outcomes of the subjective or cultural features (the professional identity items).

TABLE 8.7
Professional Opportunity Grade: Example

Professional Opportunity for Contingent Faculty	Scores
Professional development	7.50
Opportunity for advancement	8.75
Academic freedom	8.33
Section average: (7.50 + 8.75 + 8.33) ÷ 3 =	8.19
Section percentage Divide the section average by the maximum possible points. 8.19 ÷ 10 = .819 or rounded to 82%	.819 or rounded to 82%

Note. Data in this table are fictitious for visual illustration.

Calculating Professional Identity

To calculate professional identity (inclusion and job satisfaction), a survey must be administered to your contingent faculty.

When measuring job satisfaction, Judge and Klinger (2008) note that it is preferable to ask a series of items about how satisfied workers are with different dimensions of their job (e.g., "How satisfied are you with your supervisor?" "How satisfied are you with your compensation?") and collect a cumulative score rather than asking a single global item (e.g., "How satisfied are you with your job?"). Similarly, the questions in this section attempt to capture individual dimensions of job satisfaction. The responses from each contingent faculty member's survey are tallied and then averaged against the other survey responses (more on this momentarily).

All survey items are designed to accompany a Likert-type scale (Table 8.8) and begin with "Indicate your level of agreement with the following statements."

TABLE 8.8
Likert Scale Scoring

Strongly Disagree	Disagree	Undecided	Agree	Strongly Agree
1	2	3	4	5

Use the same 1 (*strongly disagree*) through 5 (*strongly agree*) options for each of the individual questions in Table 8.9.

TABLE 8.9
Survey on Feelings of Inclusion and Job Satisfaction: Example

Items	Points (1–5)
1. I feel like I was given sufficient orientation and introductions when I first began teaching here.	3.87
2. I feel like I have a sufficient sense of inclusion in the department due to features like name placards, designated work space, a Web bio, and so on.	2.11
3. I really feel like a member of an academic community in my department.	3.98
4. I feel that I am sufficiently included or invited to participate in department activities and decisions.	4.5
5. I feel like I have a fair chance of eventually becoming full-time here if I want to.	4.2
6. I am satisfied with my compensation and benefits package.	3.3
7. I am satisfied with the administrative support and resources I receive from my department to help me do my job well.	3.65
8. I am satisfied with the collegiality and respect I receive from the permanent members of the faculty in my department.	3.55
9. I am satisfied with the level of academic freedom I experience at this institution.	4.56
10. I am satisfied with the opportunities for advancement given to contingent faculty at this institution.	2.97
Total points: _(will vary)_ ÷ 10 = ____ Individual average score: _(will vary)_ Institutional average score: ___3.67___	

Note. Data in this table are fictitious for visual illustration.

Calculating a Score From Survey Responses

Step 1

Create an institutional average score by averaging each respondent's individual average score.

Step 2

Divide the institutional average score by 5 (because it is the highest possible point value). This will allow you to calculate the total survey score as a decimal and then a percentage; for example, 3.67 ÷ 5.0 = .734 or 73% (a grade of C).

Again, think of the quality of the score as parallel to grades. An A is excellent, a B is good, a C is average, a D is poor, and an F is failing.

Calculating the Total Professional Equity Grade

Finally, to calculate an overall professional equity grade, average the professional opportunity percentage (Table 8.7) with the professional identity percentage as shown in the following example:

(82% + 73%) ÷ 2 = 77.5, or rounded to 78% (C+)

Then use the academic scale to give your campus a grade of A for excellent, B for good, C for average, D for poor, and F for failing. In this example, the overall professional equity score is 78% or C+.

Calculating Gender and Racial Equity and the Overall Social Equity Grade

This section contains explanations of how to calculate gender equity, racial equity, and the overall social equity grade for the institution in question. To perform these calculations, you will need headcounts of full-time and contingent faculty, as well as their distribution by gender and race. The headcount of contingent faculty and noncontingent faculty can be obtained from your office of institutional research.

Calculating Gender Equity

Gender equity is simple to calculate.[2] An ideal score results from contingent and noncontingent faculty being 50% men and 50% women. Although exactly perfect splits are unlikely year to year, a ratio close to 50:50 is the goal. Obviously, campuses with single-gender student populations may not wish to calculate a gender equity score for their faculty. For all other campuses, use the following formula:

> Gender equity = (contingent faculty gender parity) + (noncontingent faculty gender parity)

Step 1

Identify which gender is the smaller number of contingent faculty. In other words, which group is below 50%, men or women?

Step 2

Repeat Step 1 for noncontingent or full-time permanent faculty. In other words, which group is below 50%, men or women?

Step 3

Add the gender percentages from Step 1 and Step 2, from contingent and noncontingent faculty. The sum is your final score.

For example, suppose women make up 57% of the contingent faculty, and men are 43% of the contingent faculty. The smaller number of the two would be used, in this case the male percentage of 43%. Then suppose that women are 41% of the noncontingent faculty, and men are 59%. Women are the smaller number, so use 41%. Then add the two percentages.

> 43% + 41% = 84%

Using the grading scale, 84% would be a B on gender equity.

Calculating Racial Equity

Calculating racial equity is more complicated than gender equity and must take into consideration proportions from three sources: ratios of the student population at the institution, the county, and the state. Campuses with a specific mission of service to particular ethnic groups, such as tribal colleges, are obviously exempt from the type of calculation used here. Schools simply making intentional programmatic efforts to reach particular racial groups or schools that have been given designations based on demographics (e.g., Hispanic-serving institutions) should still be included.

If student population demographics are not available on the college website, check with the institutional research office or use the College Navigator to gather the information from the NCES (nces.ed.gov/collegenavigator). County and state demographics are available at the U.S. Census Bureau website (factfinder.census.gov/faces/nav/jsf/pages/index.xhtml). The resulting

FIGURE 8.1. U.S. Census Bureau data screenshot for Florida, 2010.

HISPANIC OR LATINO AND RACE		
Total population	18,801,310[r40184]	100.0
Hispanic or Latino	4,223,806	22.5
White alone	3,224,440	17.2
Black or African American alone	148,762	0.8
American Indian and Alaska Native alone	24,193	0.1
Asian alone	9,605	0.1
Native Hawaiian and Other Pacific Islander alone	2,561	0.0
Some Other Race alone	632,682	3.4
Two or More Races	181,563	1.0
Not Hispanic or Latino	14,577,504	77.5
White alone	10,884,722	57.9
Black or African American alone	2,851,100	15.2
American Indian and Alaska Native alone	47,265	0.3
Asian alone	445,216	2.4
Native Hawaiian and Other Pacific Islander alone	9,725	0.1
Some Other Race alone	48,462	0.3
Two or More Races	291,014	1.5

Note. From U.S. Census Bureau (n.d.b.).

data look like the screenshot in Figure 8.1. This example is for Florida from the latest census, 2010. Although the census is only conducted every 10 years, updated estimates are provided periodically. If you use one of these updated estimates rather than the original census counts, be sure to indicate that choice on your final score.

The U.S. Census Bureau calculates Hispanic or Latino separately from the other racial categories. However, most colleges and universities include Hispanic or Latino in addition to all other racial categories. As a result, be sure to use the statistics from the section that looks like Figure 8.1 and use the total number for Hispanic or Latino, which in this case is 22.5%. The percentages for other racial categories appear under the subheading "Not Hispanic or Latino," below the "Hispanic or Latino" section.

For the purposes of the Contingent Labor Conditions Score the categories American Indian and Alaska Native are combined with Native Hawaiian and Other Pacific Islander because of the low percentages in each category. Similarly, Some Other Race is combined with Two or More Races.

Step 1

Make benchmark targets by averaging campus, county, and state demographics. Use Table 8.10 to find the faculty diversity benchmark goals for your campus. For each race category, add the percentages for student population, county population, and state population and divide by 3 to find the mean, which provides you with your benchmark. Rounding to two decimal places (e.g., 23.12%) will suffice from here forward.

TABLE 8.10
Race Benchmarks: Example

Race	Student Population (%)	County Population (%)	State Population (%)	Resulting Benchmark (Mean %)
American Indian and Alaska Native plus Native Hawaiian and other Pacific Islander	0.5	0.7	0.4	0.53
Asian	6.1	3.4	2.4	3.97
Black or African American	11.2	17.3	15.2	14.57
Hispanic or Latino	17.8	28.9	22.5	23.07
White	61.3	45.6	57.9	54.93
Two or more races plus some other race	3.1	4.1	1.8	3.0

Note. State data here are from the Florida census along with fictitious county and campus data for illustrative purposes.

Again, the resulting benchmarks are the percentages that your faculty demographics would meet as a goal of a faculty proportionate to and representative of the student and local populations.

Step 2

Find the actual percentages by race for contingent and noncontingent faculty as shown in Table 8.11.

TABLE 8.11
Percentages by Race for Contingent and Noncontingent Faculty: Example

Race	Contingent Faculty (%)	Noncontingent Faculty (%)
American Indian and Alaska Native plus Native Hawaiian and other Pacific Islander	0.4	0.2
Asian	4.3	8.4
Black or African American	12.6	6.7
Hispanic or Latino	19.6	15.6
White	59.3	66.9
Two or more races plus some other race	3.8	2.2

Note. Data here are fictitious for illustrative purposes.

Step 3

Find the difference between the benchmark goals and the faculty data.

Calculate contingent faculty and noncontingent faculty separately. Take the contingent faculty actual percentage and find the difference from the resulting benchmark for each category. Regardless of whether the actual percentage is over or under the benchmark, use positive numbers (absolute values) for the difference. Then add all the differences for each category for a total amount of difference. Repeat the steps with noncontingent faculty to get a total amount of difference from the benchmark goals and the actual percentages. These numbers are valuable to view separately from one another, because many campuses may appear more diverse than they really are by having a disproportionate amount of minority groups in contingent rather than noncontingent roles. See Table 8.12 for illustrative sample data.

TABLE 8.12
Differences From the Benchmarks: Example

Benchmark	–	Contingent	=	Difference		Benchmark	–	Noncontingent	=	Difference
0.53	–	0.4	=	0.13		0.53	–	0.2		0.33
3.97	–	4.3	=	−0.33		3.97	–	8.4		−4.43
14.57	–	12.6	=	1.97		14.57	–	6.7		7.87
23.07	–	19.6	=	3.47		23.07	–	15.6		7.47
54.93	–	59.3	=	−4.37		54.93	–	66.9		−11.97
3.0	–	3.8	=	−0.8		3.0	–	2.2		0.8
		Total:		11.07[a]					Total:	32.87[a]

Note. [a]Add the absolute value of the difference column, treating all the items as positive numbers.

Subtract the contingent percentages from the benchmarks first. Add up all numbers in the "Difference" column as positive numbers. In other words, use absolute value. Then follow the same process for noncontingent faculty (see Table 8.12).

Subtract the difference from 100 to get a percentage.

Contingent:

  100 − 11.07 = 88.93 or B+

Noncontingent:

  100 − 32.87 = 67.13 or D+

Step 4

Find the racial equity score.

Although these data are fictitious, they are not far from numbers common at many campuses, where race representation can differ greatly between contingent and noncontingent ranks. Average the two diversity scores for a final racial diversity score.

$$(88.93 + 67.13) \div 2 = 78.03$$

Round 78.03 down to 78%, which is a C+

Calculating the Overall Grade for Social Equity

Finally, average the gender and racial equity scores. Then place the score on the grading scale.

To use the examples from this chapter, the gender equity score was 84%, and the racial equity score 78%, which averages to a total social equity score of 81%, or a grade of B−.

Final Contingent Labor Conditions Score

The final scores tallied across each section provide a type of institutional report card, as well as a catalyst for important conversations and intentional planning about contingent labor conditions. See Table 8.13 (following page) for an illustrative example of a completed Contingent Labor Conditions Score, in this case using the example numbers from this chapter. As a reminder, blank versions of the table and the Excel version of this tool can be found on this book's accompanying website (https://sty.presswarehouse .com/books/BookDetail.aspx?productID=412424).

Notes

1. The AAUP annually collects data on faculty compensation for many campuses available from data.chronicle.com/?cid=megamenu#/id=table,
2. Understanding that gender is not always binary, gender here is intended to be whichever gender an individual most closely identifies with.

TABLE 8.13
Example: Visual Hierarchy of Contingent Labor Conditions Scores

Contingent Labor Conditions Score: 79% C+						
Material Equity Grade: 77%, C+			Professional Equity Grade: 78%, C+		Social Equity Grade: 81%, B	
Pay Parity Grade: 72%, C-	Job Security Grade: 75%, C	Benefits Grade: 83%, B	Professional Opportunity Grade: 82%, B-	Professional Identity Grade: 73%, C	Gender Equity Grade: 84%, B	Racial Equity Grade: 78%, C+
• Pay per course comparable to noncontingent faculty	• Rehire rights • Consistency of assignment • Allowance for breaks in service • Grievance process	• Medical • Retirement • Dental • Vision • Allowances for dependents	• Professional development • Opportunities for advancement • Academic freedom	• Sense of inclusion and job satisfaction	• Gender representation in proportion to population served	• Racial representation in proportion to population served

Note. The scores here are collected from the examples in chapter 8.

9

Conclusion

Higher education is not the only industry with a growing reliance on a contingent workforce. Many industries engage in the same practice but with a range of treatment, from per diem nurses, who receive relatively high compensation for their contingency, to users of platform capitalism (i.e., the various gig apps like Uber or TaskRabbit) that typically pays lower wages for piecework. Contingent faculty tend to fall in the middle of these extremes of compensation, with wide variation from campus to campus. Improvement of working conditions for contingent faculty can come from external sources, like federal or state legislation, but more commonly it comes from on-campus leaders such as campus administrators who create hiring and compensation policies or labor organizers who are able to negotiate pay and address job security grievances. In an ideal situation, the administration and faculty are able to work together for fair conditions—of course, this is not always what happens.

Most institutions become dependent on contingent labor as a way of cutting costs, yet it is not clear if contingent labor truly reduces overall costs in the long run. Administrative costs rise with fewer full-time faculty to do service work, including campus governance and student advising. If student outcomes slip, the campus may fall in rankings, leading to students taking their tuition dollars elsewhere. A similar situation exists with public funding of higher education, where less public investment in higher education may not lead to tax dollar savings in the long run. Contingent faculty are more likely to require unemployment pay between academic terms and other tax-funded social services. Despite campus and taxpayer costs, the greatest cost may well be to students with a rising proportion of their faculty less available because the contingent faculty have to rush off to another institution to teach a class. Students may find contingent faculty less prepared because they teach too many classes trying to make ends meet and cannot spend extra time on course preparation or offer more extensive feedback on student assignments.

Students may not be able to find a favorite faculty member a few terms later when seeking advising or career advice or to ask for a letter of recommendation because contingent faculty typically have shorter lengths of service at a given institution. As the data in chapter 2 illustrate, a greater proportion of contingent faculty on a given campus is even associated with lower student incomes several years later. But these are all issues that can be improved. It took four decades of steady losses in the proportion of full-time faculty to reach the present situation, and even small steps in the right direction can accumulate to large gains.

The Contingent Labor Conditions Score can help. It can provide an institutional report card to spark conversation and planning; it can also be repeated every year or two to provide longitudinal data. This allows campus leaders to chart progress and changes. The Contingent Labor Conditions Score also provides a way for campuses to compare themselves to one another, either through offices of institutional research, administrators, and faculty sharing scores or even campus labor organizers sharing or posting scores. Campuses that have higher or lower scores in particular areas can look to each other's practices for ideas and tips on how to improve their own score.

For academics who study higher education, the Contingent Labor Conditions Score can help us improve research on contingent academic labor by creating a standardized set of scores that can be correlated with other institution-level variables representing campus conditions. This will allow future research to more fully explore the relationship between contingent faculty's work conditions and student outcomes. The challenge with much of the existing literature is that each campus has different conditions. When studying the effects of contingent academic labor, there is sometimes a methodological assumption that all contingency is the same—a point this book stresses could not be further from the truth. Campuses with the worst practices see many of the worst outcomes from demoralized and overworked contingent instructors, whereas campuses with the best practices have found that non-tenure-track faculty who emphasize teaching are likely to outperform their tenured and more research-oriented peers. Although many faculty members are not thrilled about the idea of increasing numbers of full-time non-tenure-track faculty, new options should be explored that move away from the currently growing two-tier system and its ever-widening gap between tenure and contingency.

For those planning on finding their institution's Contingent Labor Conditions Score, a recommended place to start is determining if you want to find the score on all three areas covered in this guide, one of the three main areas, or a subcomponent of one of the three, which follow:

1. Material equity which is broken into scores on pay parity, job security, and benefits
2. Professional equity, which looks at opportunities for contingent faculty professional development and contingent faculty advancement or promotion
3. Social equity, which looks at inclusivity by race as well as by gender

The score is designed to function as either a composite or its disaggregated components. In all cases it uses a typical grading system, in which F is failing and A is excellent. Of course, most campuses will fall somewhere between A and F on the majority of items.[1]

Signs of progress do exist. Schmidt (2015) points to changes made at several institutions, such as the University of Oregon where contingent faculty now have renewable annual contracts, rather than simple course-to-course contracts with clearly defined criteria for promotion and higher base salaries. At Tufts University, contingent faculty received raises; were guaranteed interviews when full-time positions became available; and had the potential for up to three-year contracts, pending good performance reviews (Schmidt, 2015). In both cases, those campuses' Contingent Labor Conditions Score for material equity and professional equity would have gone up a grade. Working together, contingent faculty, noncontingent faculty, and administrators can create better working environments in higher education that will, in turn, enhance student experiences and outcomes.

Note

1. Forms for calculating a Contingent Labor Conditions Score are provided in the Appendix. Digital versions can be downloaded from www.ENTER WEB ADDRESS HERE.com

Appendix

Contingent Labor Conditions Score Blank Forms

Job Security Items

Item	None	Weak	Moderate	Strong	
Points:	0 Points	4 Points	8 Points	12 Points	
Rehire rights	None	Preferential hiring of returning instructors after 3 years (6 semesters, 9 quarters) of service	Preferential hiring of returning instructors immediately or before 3 years	Preferential hiring of returning instructors within 3 years plus allowance for multiyear renewable contracts	Points:
Points:	0 Points	1 Point	2 Points	3 Points	
Consistency of assignment	By convenience of chair or scheduler	Explicitly stated policy allowances for consistency of courses or scheduling, but not both	Explicitly stated policy allowances for consistency of courses and scheduling	Additional point if tenure-track faculty cannot override returning part-time faculty for overtime load	Points:
Breaks in service	Not allowed	Only for documented hardships, faculty must get approval for allowance, rehire rights may be partially diminished	Rare breaks in service allowed without hardship documentation, rehire rights may be partially diminished	Seniority-based system allowing occasional breaks in service without diminishing seniority	Points:

(*Continues*)

Job Security Items (*Continued*)

Item	None	Weak	Moderate	Strong	
Cancellation compensation	Not compensated	Compensated less than 50%	Compensated at 50% or higher	Additional point if a 30-plus day notification of termination is required	Points:
Grievance process	No explicitly written process	Written but no representative designated to support it	Written and human resources representative or administrator is the support contact	Written and an elected faculty or union representative is the support contact	Points:
				Total points earned:	

Benefits Items

Benefit	None	Low	Modest	High	
Points:	0	3	6	9	
Medical	Not offered or available, but employee is responsible for full cost	Available with 0%–33% of costs covered by employer	Available with 34%–66% of costs covered by employer	Available with 67%–100% of costs covered by employer	Points:
Retirement	Not offered, or available, but no contribution matching	Available, with contribution matching up to 2%	Available, with contribution matching of 3%–4%	Available, with contribution matching of 5% or more	Points:
Points:	0		1	2	
Dental	Not offered or available, but employee is responsible for the full cost		Available and costs are split between the employer and employee	Available employer covers full cost	Points:
Vision	Not offered or available, but employee is responsible for the full cost		Available and costs are split between the employer and employee	Available employer covers full cost	Points:

(*Continues*)

Benefits Items (*Continued*)

Benefit	None	Low	Modest	High	
Dependents on medical benefits	Not offered or allows dependents, but at full cost to employee		Allows dependents, partially subsidized	Allows dependents, subsidized at same rate as employee	Points:
				Total points earned:	

Professional Development

Opportunities for Contingent Faculty	0 Points	5 Points	10 Points	
1. New employee orientation	Not available	Offered by some departments	Offered to all as a centralized resource	Points:
2. On-campus workshops and training	Not available (or only about policy compliance)	Offered by some departments	Offered to all as a centralized resource	Points:
3. Funds for conference travel or professional memberships	Not available	Offered by some departments	Offered to all as a centralized resource	Points:
4. Shared governance roles	Not available	Departmental level (or lower level university task forces and committees)	University level (academic senate or other top curriculum and employment policy committees)	Points:
			Total points: _____ ÷ 4 = Total score: _____	

Opportunity for Advancement

Support Mechanisms for Advancement	0 points	5 points	10 points	
1. Statistics of past conversions from contingent to permanent roles are kept updated and available	Not available	In some cases	Consistently	Points:
2. Information is available that explains what the selection criteria will be when permanent roles open up	Not available	In some cases	Consistently	Points:
3. When new full-time positions open up, current qualified contingent faculty are given priority for an interview	Not available	In some cases	Consistently	Points:
4. There is consideration of seniority in the selection process when a permanent position becomes available	Not available	In some cases	Consistently	Points:
			Total points: _____ ÷ 4 = Total score: _____	

Academic Freedom

Available Forms of Academic Freedom for Contingent Faculty	0 points	5 points	10 points	
1. Write their own syllabi with choice of texts, assignments, and assessments	Not available	In some cases	Consistently	Points:
2. A statement on academic freedom exists in an official document (e.g., employee handbook, union contract, or campus policy)	Not available	Vaguely written	Clearly written	Points:
3. Mechanisms exist to respond to student complaints about faculty for academic reasons (e.g., lecture content or grades given)	Not available	Vaguely written	Clearly written	Points:
			Total points: _____ ÷ 3 = Total score: _____	

Feelings of Inclusion and Job Satisfaction

Strongly Disagree	Disagree	Undecided	Agree	Strongly Agree
1	2	3	4	5

Items	Points (1–5)
1. I feel like I was given sufficient orientation and introductions when I first began teaching here.	
2. I feel like I have a sufficient sense of inclusion in the department due to features like name placards, designated work space, a Web bio, and so on.	
3. I really feel like a member of an academic community in my department.	
4. I feel that I am sufficiently included or invited to participate in department activities and decisions.	
5. I feel like I have a fair chance of eventually becoming full time here if I want to.	
6. I am satisfied with my compensation and benefits package.	
7. I am satisfied with the administrative support and resources I receive from my department to help me do my job well.	
8. I am satisfied with the collegiality and respect I receive from the permanent members of the faculty in my department.	
9. I am satisfied with the level of academic freedom I experience at this institution.	
10. I am satisfied with the opportunities for advancement given to contingent faculty at this institution.	
Total points: _____ ÷ 10 = Average score: _____	

Make Benchmark Targets by Averaging Student, County, and State Demographics

Race	Student Population (%)	County Population (%)	State Population (%)	Resulting Benchmark (Mean %)
American Indian and Alaska Native plus Native Hawaiian and Other Pacific Islander				
Asian				
Black or African American				
Hispanic or Latino				
White				
Two or more races plus some other race				

Find the Percentages by Race for Contingent and Noncontingent Faculty

Race	Contingent Faculty (%)	Noncontingent Faculty (%)	
American Indian and Alaska Native plus Native Hawaiian and Other Pacific Islander			
Asian			
Black or African American			
Hispanic or Latino			
White			
Two or more races plus some other race			

Difference Between Actual and Benchmark Values for Contingent and Noncontingent Faculty

Benchmark − Contingent = Difference	
—	=
—	=
—	=
—	=
—	=
—	=
	Total:

Benchmark − Noncontingent = Difference	
—	=
—	=
—	=
—	=
—	=
—	=
	Total:

Note. Add the absolute value of the difference column, treating all the items as positive numbers.

Contingent Labor Conditions Score

Contingent Labor Conditions Score:						
Material Equity Grade:			Professional Equity Grade:		Social Equity Grade:	
Pay Parity Grade:	Job Security Grade:	Benefits Grade:	Professional Opportunity Grade:	Professional Identity Grade:	Gender Equity Grade:	Racial Equity Grade:
• Pay per course comparable to noncontingent faculty	• Rehire rights • Consistency of assignment • Allowance for breaks in service • Grievance process	• Medical • Retirement • Dental • Vision • Allowances for dependents	• Professional development • Opportunities for advancement • Academic freedom	• Sense of inclusion and job satisfaction	• Gender representation in proportion to population served	• Racial representation in proportion to population served

References

Adjunct. (2017). *Merriam-Webster's Collegiate Dictionary* (11th ed.). Retrieved from www.merriam-webster.com/dictionary/adjunct

Alexander, K., Bozick, R., & Entwisle, D. (2008). Warming up, cooling out, or holding steady? Persistence and change in educational expectations after high school. *Sociology of Education, 81,* 371–396.

Alexander, R., Jr., & Moore, S. E. (2008). Introduction to African Americans: Benefits and challenges of working at predominantly White institutions: Strategies for thriving. *Journal of African American Studies, 12,* 1–3.

Association of American University Professors (n.d.). 1940 statement on principles of academic freedom: With 1970 interpretive comments. Retrieved from https://www.aaup.org/report/1940-statement-principles-academic-freedom-and-tenure

American Federation of Teachers. (2010). *A national survey of part-time/adjunct faculty.* Retrieved from www.aft.org/sites/default/files/aa_partimefaculty0310.pdf

Armstrong, E. A., & Hamilton, L. T. (2013). *Paying for the party: How college maintains inequality.* Cambridge, MA: Harvard University Press.

Aronowitz, S. (1998). Are unions good for professors? *Academe, 84,* 12–17.

Arum, R., & Roksa, J. (2011). *Academically adrift: Limited learning on college campuses.* Chicago, IL: University of Chicago Press.

Bahr, P. R. (2008). Cooling out in the community college: What is the effect of academic advising on students' chances of success? *Research in Higher Education, 49,* 704–732.

Baldwin, R. G., & Chronister, J. L. (2001). *Teaching without tenure.* Baltimore, MA: Johns Hopkins University Press.

Berry, J. (2005). *Reclaiming the ivory tower: Organizing adjuncts to change higher education.* New York, NY: Monthly Review Press.

Berry, J., & Savaris, M. (2012). *Directory of U.S. faculty contracts and bargaining agents in institutions of higher education.* New York, NY: National Center for the Study of Collective Bargaining in Higher Education and the Professions.

Bertoncini, M. R., & Dorer, T. (2016). *Four things you should know about the adjunct faculty labor movement: School administrators must understand and address the issues at play.* Retrieved from universitybusiness.com/article/0916-adjunct

Bettinger, E., & Long, B. T. (2004). *Do college instructors matter? The effects of adjuncts and graduate assistants on students' interests and success.* Cambridge, MA: National Bureau of Economic Research.

Binder, A., & Wood, K. (2013). *Becoming right: How campuses shape young conservatives.* Princeton, NJ: Princeton University Press.

Bourdieu, P., & Passeron, J.C. (1979). The inheritors: French students and their relation to culture. Chicago, IL: The University of Chicago Press.

Bousquet, M. 2005. The faculty organize, but management enjoys solidarity. *Symplok, 13*(1/2), 182–206.

Boyer, E. L. (1990). *Scholarship reconsidered: Priorities of the professoriate.* San Francisco, CA: Jossey-Bass.

Braxton, J. M., Luckey, W., & Helland, P. (2002). *Institutionalizing a broader view of scholarship through Boyer's four domains.* San Francisco, CA: Jossey-Bass.

Brown, E. G. (2017). *2017–18 governor's budget summary.* Retrieved from www .ebudget.ca.gov/FullBudgetSummary.pdf

Buckley, W. K., Healy, D., & Ziv, N. D. (1985). Three comments on the richness of language and the poverty of part-timers. *College English, 47,* 537–540.

California Community Colleges Chancellor's Office. (2017). *Management information systems data mart.* Retrieved from datamart.cccco.edu/Faculty-Staff/Staff_ Demo.aspx

California State University. (2016). *Average salaries for full-time faculty by rank and appointment type (headcount).* Retrieved from www2.calstate.edu/csu-system/ faculty-staff/employee-profile/csu-faculty/Pages/average-salaries-for-full-time-faculty-by-rank-and-appointment-type.aspx

Carroll, J. (2003, June 23). We're exploited, not unqualified. *Chronicle of Higher Education.* Retrieved from www.chronicle.com/article/Were-Exploited-Not/22884

Clark, B. R. (1960). The "cooling-out" function in higher education. *American Journal of Sociology, 65,* 569–576.

Coalition on the Academic Workforce. (2012). *A portrait of part-time faculty members: A summary of findings on part-time faculty respondents to the Coalition on the Academic Workforce Survey of Contingent Faculty Members and Instructors.* Retrieved from www.academicworkforce.org/survey.html

Collins, R. (1979). *The credential society: A historical sociology of education and stratification.* New York, NY: Wiley.

Contingent. (2017). *Merriam-Webster's Collegiate Dictionary* (11th ed.). Retrieved from www.merriam-webster.com/dictionary/contingent

Conway, N., & Briner, R. B. (2002). Full-time versus part-time employees: Understanding the links between work status, the psychological contract, and attitudes. *Journal of Vocational Behavior, 61,* 279–301.

Corrice, A. (2009). Unconscious bias in faculty and leadership recruitment: A literature review. *Association of American Medical Colleges, 9*(2). Retrieved from www .aamc.org/download/102364/data/aibvol9no2.pdf

Cosco, F., & Longmate, J. (2012). An instructive model of how more equity and equality is possible: The Vancouver Community College Model. In A. Kezar (Ed.), *Embracing non-tenure track faculty: Changing campuses for the new faculty majority* (pp. 55–83). New York, NY: Routledge.

Cotter, D. A., Hermsen, J. M., & Vanneman, R. (2011). The end of the gender revolution? Gender role attitudes from 1977 to 2008. *American Journal of Sociology, 117*, 259–289.

Cotton, S. R., & Wilson, B. (2006). Student-faculty interactions: Dynamics and determinants. *Higher Education, 51*, 487–519.

Data from the 2016 Almanac. (2016, August 14). Retrieved from www.chronicle.com/interactives/almanac-2016#id=3_100

Davis, G. F. (2016). *The vanishing American corporation: Navigating the hazards of a new economy*. Oakland, CA: Berrett-Koehler.

DeCew, J. W. (2003). *Unionization in the academy: Visions and realities*. Lanham, MD: Rowman & Littlefield.

Deutsch, S. R. (2015). *The relationship between adjunct faculty staffing and college student retention and graduation*. Retrieved from scholarship.shu.edu/cgi/viewcontent.cgi?article=3169&context=dissertations

Dooris, M. J., & Guidos, M. (2006, May). Tenure achievement rates at research universities. Paper presented at the annual meeting of the Association for Institutional Research, Chicago, Ill. Retrieved from www.airweb.org/EducationAnd Events/AnnualConference/Documents/2006finalpgm.pdf

Dozier, R. (2014). *The experiences of faculty of color at Western Washington University*. Bellingham, WA: Western Washington University.

Eagan, M. K., & Jaeger, A. J. (2008). Closing the gate: Part-time faculty instruction in gatekeeper courses and first-year persistence. *New Directions for Teaching and Learning, 115*, 39–53.

Ehrenberg, R. G., & Zhang, L. (2005). Do tenured and tenure-track faculty matter? *Journal of Human Resources, 40*, 647–659.

England, P. (2010). The gender revolution: Uneven and stalled. *Gender and Society, 24*, 149–166.

Fantasia, R., & Stepan-Norris, J. (2007). The labor movement in motion. In D. A. Snow, S. A. Soule, & H. Kriesi, *The Blackwell companion to social movements* (pp. 555–575). Malden, MA: Blackwell.

Feldman, D. C. (1996). The nature, antecedents, and consequences of underemployment. *Journal of Management, 22*, 385–407.

Fields, M. W., & Thacker, J. W. (1991). Job related attitudes of part-time and full-time workers: A quasiexperimental study. *Journal of Managerial Psychology, 6*(2), 17–20.

Figlio, D. N., Schapiro, M. O., & Soter, K. B. (2015). Are tenure track professors better teachers? *Review of Economics and Statistics, 97*, 715–724.

Flaherty, C. (2012a, November 12). So close yet so far. *Inside Higher Ed*. Retrieved from http://www.insidehighered.com/news/2012/11/20/college-cuts-adjuncts-hours-avoid-affordable-care-act-costs

Flaherty, C. (2012b, December 4). Who deserves affordable care? *Inside Higher Ed*. Retrieved from www.insidehighered.com/news/2012/12/05/higher-education-officials-look-washington-guidance-adjuncts-and-affordable-care-act#sthash.6AXmN1wq.dpbs

Gappa, J. M. (1984). *Part-time faculty: Higher education at a crossroads*. Washington, DC: Association for the Study of Higher Education.

Gappa, J. M., & Leslie, D. W. (1993). *The invisible faculty: Improving the status of part-timers in higher education*. San Francisco, CA: Jossey-Bass.

Goffman, E. (1952). On cooling the mark out: Some aspects of adaptation to failure. *Psychiatry, 15*, 451–463.

Gulli, B. (2009). Knowledge production and the superexploitation of contingent academic labor. *Workplace, 16*, 1–30.

Hacker, A., & Dreifus, C. (2011). *Higher education? How colleges are wasting our money and failing our kids—and what we can do about it*. New York, NY: St. Martin's Griffin.

Hagedorn, L. S., Chi, W., Cepeda, R. M., & McLain, M. (2007). An investigation of critical mass: The role of Latino representation in the success of urban community college students. *Research in Higher Education, 48*, 73–91.

Hall, P. D., & Rivera-Torres, K. (2011). Student perceptions regarding the benefits of minority faculty at predominantly White colleges and universities. *Journal of Multiculturalism in Education, 7*(2), 1–17.

Hanzimanolis, M. (2013). California Community College faculty wage, salary, and parity analysis. *California Community College Journal, 15*(2), 5.

Harrison-Kahan, L. (2014, July 17). Blaming the victim: Ladder faculty and the lack of adjunct activism. *Chronicle of Higher Education, Vitae*. Retrieved from chroniclevitae.com/news/613-blaming-the-victim-ladder-faculty-and-the-lack-of-adjunct-activism

Haydu, J. (1988). *Between craft and class: Skilled workers and factory politics in the United States and Britain, 1890–1922*. Berkeley, CA: University of California Press.

Higher Education Research Institute. (2017). *HERI faculty survey*. Retrieved from heri.ucla.edu/heri-faculty-survey

House Committee on Education and the Workforce Democratic Staff. 2014. *The just-in-time professor: A staff report summarizing eforum responses on the working conditions of contingent faculty in higher education*. Washington, DC: Author.

Hutto, P. N. (2013). *A correlational analysis of course retention and faculty status in a community college setting* (Doctoral dissertation). Retrieved from http://digital commons.liberty.edu/doctoral/767

Jacoby, D. (2006). Effects of part-time faculty employment on community college graduation rates. *Journal of Higher Education, 77*, 1081–1103.

Jan, T. (2010, February 16). Colleges lagging on faculty diversity. *Boston Globe*. Retrieved from www.boston.com/news/education/higher/articles/2010/02/16/boston_area_short_on_black_hispanic_professors/?page=2

Jaschik, S. (January, 2015). Big union win. *Inside Higher Ed*. Retrieved from https://www.insidehighered.com/news/2015/01/02/nlrb-ruling-shifts-legal-ground-faculty-unions-private-colleges

Jay, K. (2004). I was an adjunct laborer in the fields of academe. *Chronicle of Higher Education, 50*(35), B7–B9. Retrieved from chronicle.com/article/I-Was-an-Adjunct-Laborer-in/5725

Jayakumar, U. M., Howard, T. C., Allen, W. R., & Han, J. C. (2009). Racial privilege in the professoriate: An exploration of campus climate, retention, and satisfaction. *Journal of Higher Education, 80*, 538–563.

Jones, L., Castellanos, J., & Cole, D. (2002). Examining the ethnic minority student experience at predominantly White institutions: A case study. *Journal of Hispanic Higher Education, 1*, 19–39.

Judge, T. A., & Klinger, R. (2008). Job satisfaction: Subjective well-being at work. In M. Eid & R. J. Larsen (Eds.), *The science of subjective well-being* (pp. 393–413). New York, NY: Guilford Press.

June, A. W. (2010, July 25). A Canadian college where adjuncts go to prosper. *Chronicle of Higher Education*. Retrieved from chronicle.com/article/A-Canadian-College-Where/123629

June, A. W., & Newman, J. (2013, January 4). Adjunct project reveals wide range in pay. *Chronicle of Higher Education*. Retrieved from chronicle.com/article/Adjunct-Project-Shows-Wide/136439

Kalleberg, A. (2011). *Good jobs, bad jobs: The rise of polarized and precarious employment systems in the United States, 1970s to 2000s*. New York, NY: Russell Sage Foundation.

Karmen, A. (1978). Comment "exchange on 'part-time' employment." *American Sociologist, 13*, 206–207.

Kezar, A. (Ed.) (2012). *Embracing non-tenure track faculty: Changing campuses for the new faculty majority*. New York, NY: Routledge.

Kezar, A. (2013). Departmental cultures and non-tenure-track faculty: Willingness, capacity, and opportunity to perform at four-year institutions. *Journal of Higher Education, 84*, 153–188.

Kezar, A., & Sam, C. (2013). Institutionalizing equitable policies and practices for contingent faculty. *The Journal of Higher Education, 84*(1), 56–87.

Kirch, D. G. (2013). Higher education in the age of Obamacare. *Trusteeship Magazine, 4*(21). Retrieved from agb.org/trusteeship/2013/7/higher-education-age-obamacare

Koma, A. (2014, April 29). Part-time faculty cope with economic hardships, lack of university support. *USA Today, College*. Retrieved from college.usatoday.com/2014/04/29/part-time-faculty-cope-with-economic-hardships-lack-of-university-support

Langston, S. M. (2006). Reflections on being an adjunct. Retrieved from www.sbl-site.org/publications/article.aspx?ArticleId=546

Lautsch, B. A. (2002). Uncovering and explaining variance in the features and outcomes of contingent work. *Industrial and Labor Relations Review, 56*(1), 22–43.

Lerner, S. (2009). Global corporations, global unions. In J. Goodwin and J. Jasper (Eds.), *The social movements reader: Cases and concepts* (2nd ed., pp. 364–370). Malden, MA: Blackwell.

Linden, R. C., Wayne, S. J., Kraimer, M. L., & Sparrowe, R. T. (2003). The dual commitments of contingent workers: An examination of contingent commitment to the agency and the organization. *Journal of Organizational Behavior, 24*, 609–625.

Marsden, P. V. (2000). Social networks. In E. F. Borgatta & R. J. V. Montgomery (Eds.), *Encyclopedia of sociology*, (pp. 2727–2735). New York, NY: MacMillan.

Maynard, D. C., & Joseph, T. A. (2008). Are all part-time faculty underemployed? The influence of faculty status preference on satisfaction and commitment. *Higher Education, 55*(2), 139–154.

McConnell, F. R. (1993). Freeway flyers: The migrant workers of the academy. In S. I. Fontaine & S. Hunter (Eds.), *Writing ourselves into the story* (pp. 40–58). Carbondale, IL: Southern Illinois University Press.

McHenry, L., & Sharkey, P. W. (2014). Of Brahmins and Dalits in the academic caste system. *Academe, 100*, 35–38.

Meyer, P., & McIntosh, S. (1999). The *USA Today* Index of Ethnic Diversity. *International Journal of Public Opinion Research, 4*, 56–58.

Milem, J. F., Chang, M. J., & Antonio, A. L. (2005). *Making diversity work on campus: A research-based perspective*. Washington, DC: Association of American Colleges & Universities.

Milner, J. M., & Pinker, E. J. (2001). Contingent labor contracting under demand and supply uncertainty. *Management Science, 8*, 1046–1062.

Mueller, B., Mandernach, B. J., & Sanderson, K. (2013). Adjunct versus full-time faculty: Comparison of student outcomes in the online classroom. *Journal of Online Learning and Teaching, 9*(3), 1–16.

Mysyk, A. (2001). The sessional lecturer as migrant labourer. *Canadian Journal of Higher Education, 31*(3), 73–92.

National Center for Education Statistics. (2016). *Digest of education statistics*. Retrieved from nces.ed.gov/programs/digest/index.asp

National Labor Relations Board v. Yeshiva University, 444 U.S. 672 (1980).

Ochoa, A. (2012). Contingent faculty: Helping or harming students? *Journal of the Professoriate 6*(1), 136–151.

O'Meara, K., & Rice, R. E. (2005). *Faculty priorities reconsidered: Rewarding multiple forms of scholarship*. San Francisco, CA: Jossey-Bass.

Patient Protection and Affordable Care Act, 42 U.S.C. § 18001 (2010).

Pikkety, T. (2014). *Capital in the twenty-first century*. Cambridge, MA: Belknap Press.

Pololi, L. H., & Jones, S. J. (2010). Women faculty: An analysis of their experiences in academic medicine and their coping strategies. *Gender Medicine, 7*, 438–450.

Public Sociology Department, George Mason University. (2013). *2013 Public sociology/contingent faculty working conditions survey*. Retrieved from contingentfaculty study.files.wordpress.com/2014/09/final-survey-instrument1.pdf

Reskin, B., & Padavic, I. (2002). *Women and men at work* (2nd ed.). Thousand Oaks, CA: Pine Forge Press.

Rhoades, G. (1998). *Managed professionals: Unionized faculty and restructuring academic labor*. Albany, NY: SUNY Press.

Rosenbaum, J. E., Deil-Amen, R., & Person, A. E. (2006). *After admission: From college access to college success*. New York, NY: Russel Sage Foundation.

Schackner, B. (2013, April 5). Colleges are hiring more adjunct professors: Plight of part-time faculty focus of steelworkers conference. *Pittsburgh Post-Gazette*. Retrieved from www.post-gazette.com/news/education/2013/04/05/colleges-are-hiring-more-adjunct-professors/201304050117

Schell, E. (1998). *Gypsy academics and mother-teachers: Gender, contingent labor, and writing instruction*. Portsmouth, NH: Boynton/Cook.

Schmidt, P. (2015, March 9). Adjunct advocacy. *Chronicle of Higher Education*. Retrieved from www.chronicle.com/article/Adjunct-advocacy-Contingent/228155?cid=cp7

Smith, D. G., Turner, C. S., Osei-Kofi, N., & Richards, S. (2004). Interrupting the usual: Successful strategies for hiring diverse faculty. *Journal of Higher Education, 75*, 133–160.

Smith, R. (2008). Legal protections and advocacy for contingent or "casual" workers in the United States: A case study in day labor. *Social Indicators Research, 88*, 197–213.

Smith, W. A., Altbach, P. G., & Lomotey, K. (Eds.). (2002). *The racial crisis in American higher education: Continuing challenges for the twenty-first century* (2nd ed.). Albany, NY: SUNY Press.

Sonner, B. S. (2000). A is for adjunct: Examining grade inflation in higher education. *Journal of Education for Business, 76*, 5–8.

Sonnert, G., Fox, M. F., & Adkins, K. (2007). Undergraduate women in science and engineering: Effects of faculty, fields, and institutions over time. *Social Science Quarterly, 88*, 1333–1356.

Standing, G. (2011). *The precariat: The new dangerous class*. New York, NY: Bloomsbury Academic.

Stevens, M. L. (2007). *Creating a class: College admissions and the education of elites*. Cambridge, MA: Harvard University Press.

Suddath, C. (2014, June 6). UCLA's Anderson School has a major woman problem. *Newsweek*. Retrieved from www.businessweek.com/articles/2014-06-06/uclas-anderson-business-school-is-inhospitable-to-women-report-finds

Took-Zozaya, S., & Reynolds, S. (2013). *A profile of Cabrillo College's adjunct faculty, spring 2013*. Retrieved from ccftcabrillo.org/news/issues/adjunctsurvey report051913.pdf

Townsend, B. K. (2009). Community college organizational climate for minorities and women. *Community College Journal of Research and Practice, 33*, 731–744.

Umbach, P. D. (2007). How effective are they? Exploring the impact of contingent faculty on undergraduate education. *Review of Higher Education, 30*, 91–123.

U.S. Census Bureau. (n.d.). *Selected economic characteristics: 2010–2014 American Community Survey 5-year estimates*. Retrieved from factfinder.census.gov/faces/tableservices/jsf/pages/productview.xhtml?pid=ACS_14_5YR_DP03&src=pt

U.S. Census Bureau. (n.d.). Profile of general population and housing characteristics: 2010. Retrieved from factfinder.census.gov/faces/tableservices/jsf/pages/productview.xhtml?src=CF

U.S. Department of Education. (2007). Final guidance on maintaining, collecting, and reporting racial and ethnic data to the U.S. Department of Education. *Federal Register, 72*(202). Retrieved from www.gpo.gov/fdsys/pkg/FR-2007-10-19/html/E7-20613.htm

U.S. Department of Education. (2016). *College scorecard data: Data insights.* Retrieved from collegescorecard.ed.gov/data

U.S. Department of Health & Human Services. (2014). *2014 poverty guidelines.* Retrieved from aspe.hhs.gov/poverty/14poverty.cfm

U.S. Department of Labor, Bureau of Labor Statistics. (2016). *Economic news release, Table 1. Work stoppages involving 1,000 or more workers, 1947–2016.* Retrieved from www.bls.gov/news.release/wkstp.t01.htm

Van Duyne, E. (2014). Why buy the cow? An open letter to full-time faculty [Web log post]. Retrieved from iwillstartthisblogimeanit.wordpress.com/2014/01/23/why-buy-the-cow-an-open-letter-to-the-full-time-faculty-of-american-colleges-and-universities

Weinberg, S. L. (2008). Monitoring faculty diversity: The need for a more granular approach. *Journal of Higher Education, 79,* 365–387.

Weiss, C., & Pankin, R. (2011). *Part-time faculty in higher education: A selected annotated bibliography.* Retrieved from digitalcommons.ric.edu/facultypublications/276

Wickens, C. M. (2008). The organizational impact of university labor unions. *Higher Education, 56,* 545–564.

Withers, J. (2016, February 1). We've always done it this way [Web log]. Retrieved from www.ethnography.com/2016/02/weve-always-done-it-this-way

Yang, S-O. W., & Zak, M. (1981). *Part-time faculty in Ohio: A statewide study.* Kent, OH: Kent State University, Office of Human Resource Utilization.

Zhu, Y. (2014, January 29). Latino faculty numbers remain low, 10 years after faculty diversity initiative. Retrieved from www.dukechronicle.com/articles/2014/01/29/latino-faculty-numbers-remain-low-10-years-after-faculty-diversity-initiative

Zobel, G. (2009, January 5). The adjuncts' mandate. *Inside Higher Ed.* Retrieved from www.insidehighered.com/views/2009/01/05/adjuncts-mandate

About the Author

Daniel Davis is a PhD candidate in sociology at the University of California, San Diego (UC San Diego), a Kauffman Foundation Dissertation fellow, half-time faculty at Point Loma Nazarene University, and a lecturer at San Diego State University. He has published articles on student college-to-career pathways in *Sociology of Education* and *Research in the Sociology of Organizations.* Davis previously researched undergraduate educational outcomes with the Center for Research on Educational Equity, Assessment and Teaching Excellence (CREATE) at UC San Diego. He has taught dozens of college courses in various settings, including private and public, community colleges and four-year universities, and online and face-to-face. Across these institutions, the range of working and learning conditions Davis encountered was vast, with the highest-paying campus offering compensation four times greater than the lowest-paying institution. Some of the positions had benefits and reasonable security of contract; others had neither. The sense of professional inclusion—through designated office space, invitations to department events, and more—was substantial at certain campuses and nonexistent at others. It was the experience of these disparate working conditions, their impact on Davis's sense of professional engagement, and their effect on his students that motivated him to write this book.